THE
SINGLES
ALMANAC

A Guide to Getting the Most Out of Being Single

THE
SINGLES
ALMANAC

A Guide to Getting the Most Out of Being Single

Jeffery Ullman

WORLD ALMANAC PUBLICATIONS   New York

Interior design: Levavi and Levavi
Cover design: Robert Anthony, Inc.

First published in 1986.

Paperback edition distributed in the United States
by Ballantine Books, a division of Random House, Inc.
and in Canada by Random House of Canada, Ltd.

Newspaper Enterprise Association ISBN: 0-911818-90-1
Ballantine Books ISBN: 0-345-32633-4

Printed in the United States of America.

World Almanac Publications
Newspaper Enterprise Association
A division of United Media
A Scripps Howard company
200 Park Avenue
New York, NY 10166

10 9 8 7 6 5 4 3 2 1

For my wife, Stephanie, who helped me realize how much fun there was to being single, but more importantly, showed me how fulfilling married life with her is.

For my son, Andrew, and daughter, Sarah, future video daters, who are loving proof of another Great Expectations success story.

Acknowledgments

My deepest acknowledgment and gratitude goes to the Members of Great Expectations. These adventurous souls have the strength of character and imagination to experiment with video dating, in spite of the questionable reputation of other dating services. As a result, I have had the opportunity to meet and interview thousands of them. Their generous and provocative accounts of the ups and downs of their singles lifestyle created the wellspring for **The Singles Almanac.**

Without the sharp eyes and ears of several staff members of the Los Angeles Centre of Great Expectations, I might not have been made aware of many individual dating experiences which G/E Members brought to their attention.

Without the prompting of my two closest friends, Steven Schmidt and Mark Oring, I might never have realized the importance of writing this book. It wasn't their nagging that got my research and writing started, but rather it was their understanding of what kind of future I wanted for myself. They knew that I wanted to expand the reach of Great Expectations. They knew that the writing of a book would bring tremendous possibilities. (It already has.)

Single life was fantastically exciting and enriching for me. And, to quote Julio Iglesias' and Willie Nelson's song: "...thanks to all the women I have known." Each one of them gave me insight that contributed to my character growth.

I wish to thank my researchers, Tricia Buttrill and Michele Warburton, who found material for me that might otherwise have gone unnoticed.

I also wish to thank The Putnam Publishing Group for granting permission to quote from THE ODDS ON VIRTUALLY EVERYTHING by the Editors of Herron House (© 1980 by Herron House), on which I relied for all the statistical "odds" included in **The Singles Almanac.**

One of the most enlightening ways to learn about sexually transmitted diseases is to contract one of these not-so-social diseases. I chose a safer course. I learned from two superb experts in the field, Dr. Stanley Bierman of the Bierman Century City Dermatology Medical Group, and Dr. V. Georges Hufnagel, Ob-Gyn in West Hollywood, California.

An illuminating method to find out more about the legal side of living together is to find yourself on one end of a litigious affair. As a formerly single man who had a L.T.A. (Living Together Arrangement), bought a condominium and a house with my girlfriend, wrote a will and even considered a pre-nuptial agreement, I was most concerned with the letter of the law. Amazingly, I made it through the legal maze intact. Too many people I know didn't. Someone who could have helped them was super-lawyer, Allan Herzlich, who consulted with me on the legal side of living together for **The Singles Almanac.**

My gratitude goes to my agent, Peter Fleming, who lived next door to a movie producer who met his girlfriend through Great Expectations. "What a great idea for a book!" he told them. As a result, Peter helped bring this book to you.

And, where would any successful author be without his trusted editors? Thank you, Rob Fitz and Beverly Jane Loo, for editing my 2,000 plus pages down to a more manageable amount. Otherwise, each dear reader would have to be a weightlifter to hold this book.

No ordinary publisher would have grasped why an almanac style book for singles was a natural. And Jane Flatt is no ordinary publisher. Her enthusiasm and support makes her a "mensch" in my book. Oh, yes, Jane is single, and very picky.

My appreciation goes especially to my sister, Dyan Ullman, who helped manage my business while I was so deeply involved writing this book. Her love and support allowed me to work with a clear mind.

Estelle Ullman, mother-partner-friend, shared with me her incredible insights into people and their relationships. Her passion for life, humor and straight talk permeates most of my writing and my life. Most writers don't share their work until their writing is finished. I am no different. Unfortunately, Estelle died from cancer, in May, 1985, and never got a chance to read what she helped make possible. Mom, wherever you are, these pages are open—as is my heart—for you to enjoy now.

Richard Schickel wrote of "The Transitional Woman" that in-between woman who helps build up the self-esteem of recently divorced men. Usually, she bears the full brunt of the newly singled man's craziness. Stephanie Sharp was my transitional woman, and there is no doubt in my mind that she suffered quietly and with dignity my transition from married to single man. Stephanie allowed me to "use her" to verbalize my gut-level feelings and changes, thereby helping me come to know myself better.

Schickel's "Transitional Woman" almost never ends up marrying her man. Stephanie and I were married on Valentine's Day, 1981. We defied the odds and are that much happier for it. Thank you, Stephanie, for joining Great Expectations and letting me meet you.

Contents

Introduction

What would *you* do if you were the head of a singles introductory business where many of your clients had fascinating, provocative and enlightening war stories to tell about life as a single? Find a way to collect their experiences and ideas in order to share their collective wisdom with others who might be interested! **The Singles Almanac** is the providential result of this unique opportunity.

I didn't study "Video Dating 101" at college. (To my knowledge no university gives any serious academic consideration to the very real problems of being single in the 1980s.) My research was conducted in the singles' "trenches."

For years, my standard advice after hearing many friends of all ages complain about their problems in meeting other quality, eligible single people was, "Try a new singles bar," or, "How would you like to meet a really nice friend of mine?" The response thrown back at me almost always ranged from disdain to horror. Finally, after years of being beseiged, I founded Great Expectations, a video dating service, on Leap Year's Day, 1976.

Video dating seemed an appropriate response to the problems of modern day courtship dilemmas because it allowed the individual, without any middleman matchmaker, to pre-screen potential partners and select for him- or herself the most desirable person. Although it is not the only response, it was a fitting application of my sixties' personal creed: "Power to the people!" THE SINGLES ALMANAC gives the power of information to single people everywhere.

So, dear reader, by the time you are finished reading THE SINGLES ALMANAC, you will have received the (some of the) accumulated knowledge of thousands of singles before you. You may be single, but you are definitely not alone!

1

The Singles Lifestyle

sin.gle, adj. *(from Latin singulus, meaning only one).*
1a: not married; b: of or relating to celibacy. 2: unaccom-
panied by others: LONE, SOLE. 3a (1): consisting of or
having only one part, feature, or portion; b: consisting of
one as opposed to or in contrast with many. 4a: consisting
of a separate unique whole: INDIVIDUAL.

What do you mean when you say you are single? Webster's Ninth New Collegiate Dictionary offers
you positive and negative possibilities; it is up to you to select a definition. Your choice—like the decision to call a
half-glass of water half full or half empty—will reveal
your attitude about yourself and your situation.

Being single may mean simply not being married. Or
you may feel it is a state of loneliness and emptiness. But
you may also look at it as a fascinating state in which you
can explore yourself, take advantage of the myriad opportunities life presents, and participate as a unique, whole
individual.

Being single also carries a variety of connotations, and
coming to terms with them is often the greatest struggle.
Ours is a society that has for a long time maintained an
unwritten social code: to be fulfilled one must be coupled.
From this follows that to be without a mate is to be unful-
filled; lacking in some vital resource; deficient. If you buy

into this code or its tenets they are likely to become reality for you. Being single will mean you have a long list of demons to battle.

But if you believe being single is the freedom to explore your own individual nature, you will not have to battle those attitudes. You will find you have advantages in many situations over those who are married or part of a couple. By embracing your singleness, you will open yourself to others. Being single is different in style and mood and character from being coupled, and your attitude about it can attract and encourage contact with others.

Learning to be successfully single means exploring the path of self-reliance. It means accepting responsibility for your own views, your own welfare, your own decisions. It means letting yourself be filled with passionate interests, and becoming—and believing you are—a person worth knowing.

If you find yourself continually struggling with your singleness, ask yourself if the battle is between yourself and another or if the battleground really lies inside you. Friends may come and go, lovers may fade into the ethereal land of memory, but your relationship with yourself is the one that remains. The single person has to have a special internal relationship. When the advantages of personal freedom seem to run dry, when loneliness haunts your days, when being responsible only to yourself is too heavy a burden, learn to tap another dimension of yourself. Do not allow yourself the illusion that the responsibility belongs to another.

A single person balances his focus on the inner and outer selves. Too much attention to internal realities can isolate you from social ties. But if you always focus on others, the way you see yourself will become blurred, and you will end up feeling uncertain and anxious. Living single successfully demands that you account for your assets and liabilities and invest in yourself in a big way. Once the commitment is made, the possibilities are limitless; you supply the energy and raw materials, and you reap the rewards. But to begin, you must discover your own inner voice.

How To Be Happily Single

Your autonomy will let you explore many facets of yourself, but you must first make a commitment to discovery and honesty. You have to admit to yourself that you have strengths and then you must develop them. You must listen to yourself and learn to discover that inner voice. A number of psychologists suggest that discovery of an actual inner voice can help put you in touch with yourself. Reading aloud and allowing yourself to listen to yourself helps you become aware of your range of emotions and style of communicating. Choose a book or play that you like and set aside time to read aloud for fifteen minutes each day until you finish it. Play with the words, experiment with your voice, change the speed at which you read—let your voice sing out whatever those words elicit from the emotional you. You will have fun and will find that, with time, you will begin to reach the self that you usually do not dare open in social situations. As you become comfortable with the unfolding of your secret self, you will become more creative, and it will be easier for you to see the qualities hiding in the recess of others. You will begin to allow relationships to develop gradually—like a ballet—and will learn the essence of good timing: letting a relationship develop at its own pace.

Keeping a journal can help you discover resources locked inside you. Writing down what happens each day lets you physically and emotionally re-experience events

5

and the way you responded to them. The process brings a new sense of value to a life that once may have seemed empty. In keeping a journal, you will recall with your pen past experiences—times of ecstasy and anguish, hope and despair, crises and turning points, failures and successes. Over time, you will begin to understand what many events portended and what they prepared you for. You will begin to see a thread that connects the past to the present and future.

To begin is simple. Buy a blank book—the kind with a sewn binding that you cannot tear pages from. Then make time each day to write about your adventures. Do not merely list events that take place; discuss what you think about the people and situations in your life. Focus on feelings and behavior that mean the most to you. After a while, begin to read over what you have written. If you have followed through with your commitment, you will have a record of the inner and outer aspects of your life, a history of yourself. You may notice that what happens is actually less important than your attitude to events. And that things do not just happen: you make them happen with the choices, conscious and unconscious, that you make. You may notice that self-destructive tendencies—choosing partners who cannot give you what you want and need, or moving toward someone who is superficially attractive but lacking substance underneath, for example—form patterns; the journal can help you notice them, understand their origin, and learn how to break them.

It is important for singles to fill their needs for relaxation and exercise. Living produces stresses and tension, and the body soaks these up like an enormous sponge, affecting you mentally, emotionally, and ultimately, physically. Making time every day to relax, to stretch your muscles, will relieve the body and soul of the day's anxiety.

Disciplines such as Hatha yoga can provide stretching and relaxing necessary to keep body and mind healthy. Fifteen minutes of yoga on a daily basis can release tension and give tone to muscles. When you pinpoint where tension accumulates in your body, you can choose posture exercises that can help. Hatha yoga teaches you to relax, slow down, to pay attention to the self that resides inside the body.

Jogging can also bring you into contact with inner processes. If you pay attention to what is going on around you when you jog instead of dwelling on the day's traumas, you can achieve the meditative relaxation that yoga provides. You will also increase your energy level and endurance. Meditation can be used to release stress, reduce anxiety, and combat loneliness. Practiced regularly for a few minutes each day, it can eliminate some of the pressure of daily life.

Your social self needs attention too. Social accessibility is really an attitude. It depends on generosity of spirit—whether you make yourself available to others and are open to new situations or find ways to avoid what is unfamiliar. Your relationships right now say something about your attitude. Do you reach out to others in your life? Do you make them feel special? Do you let them feel important to you?

Make a list of the most important people in your life. Are you in direct contact with them? If they are within calling or visiting distance, do so. If not, write letters. A letter is a physical and emotional act; it is an expression of yourself and your caring about another person. Letter writing is an art; it takes time, thought, and a poetic heart to find words for what you want to communicate. A good letter is a great gift to the one who receives it.

Looks do count—but attractiveness depends on something other than physical attributes. The woman or man who expresses a natural grace, a sense of style, and self-confidence turns people's heads. An attractive person radiates passion and wholeness.

As you reach out to others more and more, you will begin to exude a kind of quiet strength that makes you attractive. Others begin to seek you out as they sense that you have an ability to give, and that you will acknowledge what is special about them. Do not assume or expect things from those people. Let them reach out at their own pace, according to their own rhythm. People respond in their own time.

The facet of you that connects you with society needs exercise and practice, too. Make contact with a political group or community association. What you choose to involve yourself in depends on your interests, free time, and financial situation, but the object is to get involved with the world in a non-business way. Exercising this part of your self reminds you that you are part of a group much larger than your circle of family, friends, and co-workers.

Many people in this money-oriented, success-oriented society would have mentioned finances sooner in the discussion of being happily single. There is a popular belief that if the financial self is functioning well, the other aspects of the human being will pretty much take care of themselves. Actually, the opposite is true. When you develop the other aspects of yourself, all your talents and skills will work for you: you will be healthier, better able to concentrate, have more patience and endurance, work well with others. Then the financial self will be able to function well.

Discover your creative self. Then find a field that will make use of your talents. Establish yourself in an environment that nourishes you, that encourages the skills and talents that you want to develop. Seek reasons to excel in what you do; always put in your best effort and you will find financial security alone will not dictate your job choice, that simply paying your bills and meeting your obligations is not enough.

Invest in yourself; self-sufficiency will follow. Then you will have something to offer as a worker, as a friend, and as a partner in an emotional relationship. Your relationships will benefit from your knowledge, abilities, interests, and passionate attitude.

Alternative Lifestyles

The path to tomorrow may lead away from that venerable institution, the nuclear family. But where is it heading? Will we all be single in the year 2000?

Not likely. The prophets are promising us a cornucopia of possibilities, of which singlehood is one. In the past, most everyone married when they left home. That's still true for a lot of us today. But by the turn of the century, singlehood may be an almost mandatory period of life, a "transitional living phase" between life with parents and life with a spouse. This period will be necessary if anyone is to make an intelligent choice among the bewildering kaleidoscope of kinship situations. Sociologist Jessie Bernard figures: "The most characteristic aspect of marriage in the future will be precisely the array of options available to different people who want different things from their relationships with each other."

What are some of these options? In *Beyond Monogamy*, Robert Rimmer, also author of *The Harrad Experiment* and other futuristic sociosexual novels, proposes a corporate Future Families of America foundation to support experimental marriages. All participants in these mergers, including children, would be shareholders. Specifically, Rimmer urges subsidized menages a trois, two-and three-couple families with children, and "love groups" consisting of up to six couples of all ages.

Threesomes, he argues, "might not only extend the sex

lives of older persons into their seventies but would provide the environment for two socially approved marriages within one's lifetime." Quartets and sextets would "not only eliminate old-age loneliness, but would keep their members out of senior citizen centers and nursing homes." Love groups, as portrayed in his novel *Love Me Tomorrow*, would provide comfort and security for the elderly and, with members pooling their assets, a higher material living standard for all.

Is Rimmer just a dreamer? His visions seem tame next to a real-life extended family in California called Morehouse. Morehouse, which has been operating in the black both financially and emotionally since 1967, consists of a twenty-four-member "family" in Oakland (eight couples, some married and some not, plus children) and more than one hundred intertwined bodies and souls in nearby Lafayette. All the adults make sexual love every day, most with more than one partner. The venture is so financially successful that recently Morehouse set up property trusts for all of its children.

Communes such as Morehouse are one way we are headed, says futurist Alvin Toffler. In *The Third Wave*, he considers "aggregate families" of two divorced couples and their children, homosexual marriages, contract marriages, serial marriages, "family clusters" like Rimmer's and Morehouse, bands of elderly people and bigamist bonds between several husbands and one wife. ("That could happen if genetic tinkering lets us preselect the sex of our children, and too many parents choose boys.") Of course, all of these variations exist already. Toffler suggests they will compete with the nuclear family as choices.

A monumental change of lifestyle also lies around the corner, Toffler notes: a shift from the office back home. When husband and wife are both under the roof of the "electronic cottage," the male-female connection will become more like it was before the Industrial Revolution when "working together assured, if nothing else, tight, complex, 'hot' personal relationships—a committedness many people envy today." This may transform family relationships. "It could provide a common set of experiences and get marriage partners talking to one another again."

And it might change what we look for in the opposite sex, says Toffler. Pre-industrial "first wave" brides and grooms-to-be sought good workers, healers, teachers for their children. Second wave folk (our parents, some of us) wanted companionship, sex, warmth, support, "love." Our children (and maybe we too?) may insist on "Love Plus—sexual and psychological gratification plus brains . . . love plus conscientiousness, responsibility, self-discipline, or other work-related virtues."

Or, as California guru Swami Kriyanada advises his flock, never marry anyone you wouldn't choose as a business partner.

And don't rush too quickly to tie the knot. Who knows what you might miss out on?

You Are Not Alone

Why are so many people single? Why are there more than twice the number of singles today as there were in 1970? What factors cause 13 percent of all women and 20 percent of all men to steer clear of that venerable institution, marriage?

Ask a sociologist and he will tell you that the size of the baby-boom generation is the problem. As a group, we're much too large for our own good. There are more of us than there are opportunities for success. And when we can't succeed unless we fight for a decent place on the economic ladder, we're fighting to maintain our self-worth. If we don't have self-worth, we don't have a feeling of well-being, which is critical to making us comfortable enough to settle down and get married.

Other issues that help explain this ever-increasing phenomenon are education, housing, the attitudinal differences of the last three decades, and the women's movement.

First, education. The more education people have, the longer they wait to marry. The baby-boomer generation is the best educated generation yet, and we've got fewer marriages.

Housing being so expensive forces us to find alternatives to living on our own. Since 1970, there's been an 85 percent increase in people moving back home with their parents. This saves money, but keeps us children longer. Doubt this? Just think of the last time you were with your parents. No matter how hard you tried to show your folks the maturity and sophistication you've worked so hard to attain, bet you felt about six or seven, thirteen at best, after about five minutes in their presence.

Then there's the change in attitudes since the fifties. During the reign of conservatism, the family was the most important thing in life. No wonder people settled down and had babies at such young ages.

Everything turned topsy-turvy in the sixties. Those turbulent times, with the protests for civil rights and against Vietnam (not to mention nearly everything even remotely capitalistic) changed everything. All of a sudden, the old ways were wrong. Marriage was wrong. Family was wrong. Issues were what counted. The good of the group was what mattered most.

And as if we didn't have enough trouble reconciling these two extreme attitudes, along came the seventies, the "Me decade": self-absorption as a reaction to the other-directed sixties. It's a wonder any one of us has married at all.

Complicating matters even further was the women's movement, which told women that their place could also be in the working world, not only the home—and, in fact, contributed to helping some women feel terrible for even *thinking* about being a wife and a mother. So, women poured into the workforce, putting their careers first and letting their romantic lives slide.

A plus of starting a career is that women have become more independent. They don't need marriage for the same financial reasons they used to. They can support themselves quite well. And they do, in droves.

Now, as the biological clock ticks away, women are questioning what they did with all that time. Not that they haven't gotten rewards from their careers, it is just that they're starting to realize that they want more from life than that.

Take Joan, for example, thirty-six, never married, longing to start a family, but seeing the prospects slim and time running out.

"Okay, so I'm over thirty-five. Is that a crime or something? Maybe a disease like leprosy? All the guys I meet are looking for young little things who won't pressure them about marriage or commitment. Not that I ever say anything, but with me, I don't know, they just get scared and run away. It's that 'I won't grow up' attitude they've got. I guess they figure if they don't do any of the grown-up things like getting married and having babies, maybe they won't get older.

"I don't know. I'm getting real tired of going out on dates, too. That whole, 'Hi, I'm Joan, who are you' garbage you have to go through with every new person you meet. I've been doing this for twenty years now, and I'll tell you, it's getting a little old.

"Then when you do go out, what do these guys want? Not a relationship, that's for sure, 'cause if you don't sleep with them by the third date, that's it, you're history. It's like sex first, then we'll talk. I'm tired of waking up next to someone and having nothing to say to him.

"Maybe it's too much to ask for, having a career and a family. Yet I've got friends who are on their second marriages. Sometimes I want to scream, 'It's not fair, I haven't even had my first turn yet.'

"Maybe I should just give up. Say, 'Okay, I'll never find

anybody' and just resign myself to never being married. Being single for the rest of my life might not be so bad. Look at all the nonsense I won't have to put up with. And I'll get to do whatever I want, whenever I want, not having to answer to anyone. Being single could be just great.

"But, boy, I always thought I'd be a wonderful mother."

Then there's Susan, also thirty-six, with a completely different tale to tell.

"Oh, sure. I've almost been married, a bunch of times. I don't know what it is, but whenever I get really close to someone, something inside me snaps. I start noticing things about him, little things that drive me absolutely crazy. How could I live with someone like that? The answer is, I can't. So I bolt, or pull back, or whatever. And there goes yet another promising relationship.

"I don't think I'm looking for perfection. I mean, I know every relationship is a compromise, I don't know what is. That much compromise I don't want. But I don't think I'm asking for anything more than I'd be willing to give myself.

"I think I just haven't found Mr. Right yet. There've been guys who I've thought were right. For about six weeks, maybe three months. Then the real them comes out. Maybe we have a disagreement. Maybe two. Who needs that? I want a relationship where we won't fight.

"Besides, I've got plenty of time. Did you know the age thirty-five was purely an arbitrary statistic, in terms of danger for having babies? Sure, way back in the fifties, when the doctor was asked when it stopped being safe, he just took a wild guess. Thirty-five must have seemed pretty old back then, so that's what he said. So you see, there's no rush. And that's if I even want to have kids. I'm not sure I'd be willing to give up my freedom. Not yet, anyway. Does that sound terrible?"

Granted, Joan and Susan are two extremes, but no matter what your attitude about marriage is, just keep in mind, as a single American, you're in good company. You may be single, but you're not alone.

Changing Sex Roles In Dating

The dramatic shift in stereotyped sex roles that has occurred over the past two decades has weakened the venerable rule of courtship that the woman must patiently and passively wait for the man to ask her for a date. At least that is the theory.

In practice, today's woman still confesses anxiety at the prospect of asking a man for a date. Modern women fear that their behavior will be interpreted as brash or aggressive. They think that asking a man out is "chasing" him or "throwing" herself at him.

Thus, the same socialization processes that dictated the passive role in dating to single women of generations past are currently working to inhibit otherwise "now" females from shedding that role. Women of today find that the dating rules and rituals that they learned as teenagers are still viable: asking a man for a date invariably produces anxiety and more often than not, fails to produce the desired results.

Some women who, anxiety and fear be damned, have called a man to ask for a date have seen the man agree, but later break the date, or promise to call and then remain incommunicado. On the other hand, some men re-

15

count fulfilling relationships that would never have been had the woman not pursued them.

Although end results vary, most men confess that they enjoy the flattery and ego gratification of being asked out. Insofar as the woman is looking for a date and not an opportunity to flatter a man's ego, however, it is helpful to understand some factors that explain why men are often reluctant to assimilate the change in dating sex roles.

The stress that men experience as a result of sex role reversal dovetails with other fears that males find particularly stressful. Men fear failure, job stress, vulnerability, and emasculation. They also fear that their power, success, and achievement needs will not be fulfilled. And men fear lack of intimacy and sexual fulfillment, as much as they fear lack of affection and emotional gratification.

These stress-producing fears contribute to the man's need to be in control of a relationship. When the dominant role is threatened, as it may be when a woman takes the initiative to ask a man out, the man experiences anxiety.

And, just as men fear losing dominance and control, women fear rejection by men. The teenage dating socialization process mandates coquettish, exaggerated female behavior. It is really the fear of male rejection that produces the sex role reversal anxiety in women.

While all this seems to point to a web of irreconcilable social and psychological factors which interplay to keep men and women locked into the traditional sex roles, there is a silver lining. By opening the option of the active role in dating to women, assertive women who are willing to take the risk of asking a man out reveal themselves to men who are equally committed to breaking away from the dominance-and-control posture. A truly liberated male is genuinely impressed with a woman who is willing to pursue her interest in him and is ultimately a more satisfactory partner than the man whose self-image is more image than self.

Overcoming
The Love Junkie Syndrome

No one wants to be lonely. But being single and alone does not automatically mean (in most instances, and for most emotionally healthy people) that you have to be lonely. All of us from time to time become consumed by the desire and need to be with someone—and preferably, in a reciprocal, meaningful relationship. But for some people all of the time and for all of us some of the time, we become addicted to the overwhelming need to find someone, *anyone* to be with.

The phenomenon of being a junkie for love is not limited to single women over thirty—although this group until recently had the exclusive listing because they were raised (read "brainwashed") from infancy to believe that unless they were married, they were imperfect, failures, and less than whole. They had to stand in the shadow of their husband's protection and success and their children's accomplishments. Today, all singles and both sexes sometimes suffer (temporarily or chronically) from the affliction known as the Love Junkie Syndrome. If there isn't at least one romantic interest in their lives, they .are depressed and starved for companionship, attention, and sharing.

Liberation and raised consciousness have permeated

everyone's life. Thus, very young singles as well as the older single who suddenly finds himself or herself alone are just as likely to be affected.

Many of today's singles will swear vociferously that they like the freedom, the independence, the variety, and the lack of responsibility that their solitary status affords them. These people don't want to get serious (much less married!) *no matter what*! Yet even these staunch defenders of the playboy/playgirl lifestyle get lonely sometimes ...and sometimes, the advantages and joys of being single and free become less satisfying. Their lives seem to lack meaning, direction, and the comfort of having someone special with whom to share their accomplishments and disappointments. Playing the field *is* fun and can be a marvelous experience—at least most of the time. But even the most wild and carefree among us find this merry-go-round ride a bit boring or meaningless sometimes. In a word, even the most devout single sometimes gets lonely and wants something more—and that something is often a steady, loving relationship.

Some love junkies fall into the "ain't I a poor thing" category. They become dependent on the pity of others to whom they're quick to complain that they are in despair, have the worst luck, will never, ever fall in love again—nor will anyone ever fall in love with them even if they live to be a hundred. This attitude sometimes becomes a self-fulfilling prophecy: a bad attitude is not a way of endearing or attracting anyone to you. And the more depressed and rejected you feel, the less likely you are to be appealing to anyone else. No one wants to stay in touch with a constant whiner. This pitiful love junkie may have the body of an Adonis or the self-indulgent flab of a compulsive eater but be they beautiful or dumpy, the fact remains that they're wallowing in self-pity and self-hatred and self-destruction so deep that they *won't* find the mate of their choice for as long as they stay submerged.

Some men—but a greater number of women—simply cannot live without someone else to lean on. These lonely people may be searching for a mother image, a father image or simply the constant companionship of another person but whatever it is they're trying to achieve, the fact is they cannot be whole or happy unless they've got someone around to supplement their own lack of self-worth.

Jerry, a very well-to-do businessman, is a classic but extreme example. Perhaps his utter dread of being alone——for as short a time as one night—stems from the fact that he was orphaned at age seven. Or perhaps Jerry would have been insecure and unable to cope with himself even if that hadn't been the case. Whatever his reasons, Jerry will do *anything* to make sure he doesn't have to spend a single night alone. His black book of phone numbers is only slightly less thick than the Manhattan telephone directory and his calls to women are pitiful. He'll promise dinner, jewelry, trips to exotic places, drugs, flowers, anything at all just to insure himself a partner for the evening. He's already been married five times at the age of thirty-four, and yet has never had a healthy relationship with a woman despite his track record of being one of the Great Playboys of the Western World. He'd rather be used by women (and he knows many of them just take him for the expensive dinners, jet-set whirlwind tours and cocaine, 'ludes, and grass) in exchange for someone to sleep beside him at night. He's so afraid of being alone that he doesn't even necessarily have to have sex: he just wants a live teddy bear to comfort him.

Not only is Jerry's example an extreme one, but what makes it even more unusual is that this degree of insecurity is rare among women — and even more rare among men. Most men and women who are love junkies will manifest their dependency in less extreme ways. However, the need to be with someone, to be needed, to lean, to be loved or at least placated can show itself in many other ways. Two other common ways are for the dependent love junkie to become a marshmallow, a will-o-the-wisp with no "backbone" who molds him- or herself into anything the partner wants with little or no regard for his or her own needs and desires; or, similarly, becomes a "punching bag," a masochist who'll endure any insult or injury to spirit or dignity in exchange for attention and companionship.

Whenever men and women see love as the supreme ful-fillment, it is logical for them to search for their partner in order for them to have a sense of unity which they feel they cannot experience by themselves. For example, a woman who feels addicted to love is often attracted to a man who seems strong and superior. Sometimes she is so self-effacing that she feels that she is somehow prohibited from asserting herself. She longs for this man to "sweep her off her feet"; a passion she knows she cannot create herself.

In other words, when you're a love junkie, you cannot achieve self-fulfillment on your own. Your self-respect and self-esteem don't rest within yourself—which is where these traits belong—but rather in the reflected glo-ries (real or imagined) of someone else's life. A love junkie is a "ghost" of real life, a dependent rather than a self-re-alized man or woman. As a love junkie, you wait for a Knight In Shining Armour or Gracious and Bountiful Lady to rescue you, take away the responsibilities of taking care of yourself and making important and even trivial life decisions, (such as what to have for dinner, where to go on vacation, and the like) *for* you. The most important thing for a love junkie to remember is that even Knights and Bountiful Ladies soon tire of their burden of playing "rescuer" and "handmaiden" and "leaning post." This, in turn, will make you even more frustrated and unhappy.

As John Lennon and Yoko Ono wrote, "Life is what hap-pens to you while you're busy making other plans." And life does change. The very definition of life is change. And change is scary. However, while you're making plans to pull yourself out of the grasp of being addicted to ro-mance, to finding oneself via someone else, it's a good idea to remember that being alone does not mean you have to be lonely. Being single does not mean that you're a failure or that you're less than whole because you're alone. The key to ridding yourself of this addiction to love is learning to really like *and* love yourself. As an indepen-dent person who can rely on himself or herself without needing constant "fixes" of love, you'll soon discover that being overly dependent has, in the past, driven away more

people than it has attracted to you. You can look back-
—but only to help you profit from your former reliance on
others. No one ever said that being able to stand on your
own two feet would be easy, but no one will deny that it's
the only cure (and salvation) for any and all love junkies.

QUIZ: ARE YOU A LOVE JUNKIE?

1. Did your childhood instill in you the idea that you cannot be a "real" person who's secure *unless* you're involved in a romance, marriage, or deep love affair?
2. Have you been unable to shake off those childhood teachings of dependency?
3. Do you become anxious and frustrated when you have no love relationship or the one you're involved in is not going well?
4. Are you afraid to be alone with yourself and your own thoughts?
5. Are you unable to make decisions about your life? Would you rather make no decisions at all and hope external forces will decide for you?
6. Are you envious and jealous of people who have a happy relationship?
7. When you are involved in a relationship, are you a green-eyed jealous monster—and one who is obsessive about not letting the other person out of your sight and control?
8. Do you often (or always) feel hostile or persecuted or both?
9. Do you feel you won't be accepted unless you have a date or a lover?
10. Do you usually set unrealistic goals for yourself?
11. Do you get excited more by failure than by success? Are you afraid to make meaningful accomplishments?
12. Do you feel helpless and like a baby instead of like an adult who's in control?

13. Do you still hold on to the dream of being rescued by a Knight In Shining Armor or a Gracious and Bountiful Lady?
14. Do you think you're a will-o-the-wisp or a wimp others can take advantage of?
15. Do you usually go around feeling sorry for yourself and feeling dejected and unloved?

If the majority of your answers are "yes" to the above questions, chances are you've got a case of "Love Junkism."

OVERCOMING THE LOVE JUNKIE SYNDROME

1. Learn to love and like yourself. If you don't, no one else will like you either. Get counseling if you can't do it yourself.
2. Be your own best friend. Expect the most from yourself not the least—and above all, don't be afraid to succeed.
3. Realize you will make mistakes in judgment, that some of your decisions won't turn out as you expected: no one is ever 100 percent right. Remember, you'll learn from these mistakes.
4. By whatever means, build up your self-confidence and a good self-image. You'll be much happier with yourself—and far more attractive to others.
5. Be honest with yourself. Rely on gut feelings, not habits, and keep your fantasies for your dream life, not your everyday activities.
6. Correct your faults slowly but surely. You don't have to become perfect overnight. Being a better, more emotionally healthy person won't happen in an instant, but it is a goal well worth striving for.
7. Believe in yourself. You'd never have gotten this far if you weren't a good person in many ways.

8. Take control of your life. Even the toughest decisions will appear in perspective if and when you confront them head-on.

9. Ask others for advice, but make the final decisions yourself. No one can live your life for you.

10. Try to channel your energies positively. Try helping others, rather than wallowing in self-pity. Remember, what you keep diminishes, what you give away comes back.

11. Sometimes you will be rejected or fail. It happens to each of us. Learn to rely on yourself in these times.

The Facts

What do the statistics have to tell us about being single? They suggest that women start to outnumber men by the time they reach their twenty-fourth year. There are almost one million more single women between the ages of twenty-five and thirty-five than there are single men that age. Between the ages of thirty and fifty-four there are one and half million more single women than men. Broken down by age group, the figures show 93 men for every 100 women between the ages of twenty-five and thirty-five; 100 single men for every 132 single women between the ages of forty and forty-four; and 100 single men for every 147 single women between the ages of forty-five and fifty-four.

The obvious imbalance between the sexes is in part due

to the tendency of women to outlive men by an average of 7.7 years. A second factor is what has been popularly called "the baby boom." Women at present in their thirties find themselves part of a generation in which they vastly outnumber their male counterparts.

Interestingly, the numbers say that the bright, articulate, successful woman in America is probably living alone. Current trends show that 51.2 percent of all entering college freshmen (1984) were women. In 1970 there were 358,000 women between the ages of twenty-five and thirty-four living alone. By 1984, that figure had climbed to 1,079,000—an increase of over 301 percent!

•

WHEN DO SINGLES FEEL THE MOST LONELY?

When do you seem to feel the loneliest? Here are some of the most frequently mentioned times, listed in order of frequency.

1. Holidays
2. Birthdays
3. Sunday afternoons
4. Mealtimes—especially dinner
5. After work
6. Before going to sleep
7. At weddings
8. At parties
9. During times of illness
10. In strange cities

•

HOW SINGLES GET OVER THEIR LONELINESS

Here are some things singles have found help to provide comfort when loneliness visits.

1. Call a friend
2. Work (business-related)
3. Watch television

4. Go to a bar or nightclub
5. Work on a hobby
6. Visit a friend
7. Garden or do household chores
8. Read a book or magazine
9. Go shopping
10. Take a walk or drive
11. Exercise
12. Take a bath or shower
13. Listen to music
14. Write a letter to a friend
15. See a movie
16. Think or meditate

•

WHAT SINGLES SAY THEY FEAR MOST

Hundreds of single people throughout the United States were asked to name their greatest fears as a single person. Here are the results.

1. Not finding the right person for me
2. Finding the right person and then discovering that that person was not really so "right" after all
3. Wondering how well my children will adapt to being raised by one parent
4. Wondering if he will call me
5. Worrying that she will turn me down
6. Anxiety about being attractive to the opposite sex (usually following a divorce or death)
7. Wondering what to do now (usually a fear of a newly single person who has not been dating for a long time)
8. Saying the wrong thing at the wrong time, for example, calling your partner by the wrong first name in the middle of lovemaking

•

FEARS OF SINGLE WOMEN

A recent survey asked single women to name their greatest fears. The sobering results of that survey are below.

1. Fear for personal safety
2. Fear of physical injury
3. Fear of loss of identity
4. Fear of growing old
5. Fear of financial insecurity
6. Fear of loneliness
7. Fear of failure
8. Fear that no one cares

WHO IS SINGLE AFTER AGE SIXTY-FIVE?

	Men	Women
Never Married	4.5%	5.7%
Married	79.3%	39.4%
Widowed	12.8%	51.3%
Divorced	3.4%	3.6%

Source: U.S. Department of Commerce.

THE TEN MOST DESIRED PHYSICAL QUALITIES

What women look at in men
1. Smile
2. Eyes
3. Laugh
4. Weight
5. Height
6. Hair
7. Buttocks
8. Legs
9. Muscles
10. Chest

What men look at in women
1. Smile
2. Eyes
3. Weight
4. Legs
5. Breasts
6. Laugh
7. Hair
8. Buttocks
9. Mouth
10. Stomach

THE TEN MOST DESIRED PERSONALITY QUALITIES

What women look for in men
1. Sense of humor
2. Honesty
3. Intelligence
4. Sensitivity
5. Dependability
6. Understanding
7. Integrity
8. Affection
9. Ambition
10. Sexiness

What men look for in women
1. Sense of humor
2. Affection
3. Sexiness
4. Intelligence
5. Sensitivity
6. Honesty
7. Understanding
8. Integrity
9. Charm
10. Ability to listen

II

Meeting People

Where To Find Each Other

If you're female, over thirty and live on the East coast, give up. Okay, maybe it's not that bad, but your chances of marriage aren't nearly as good as those of someone younger, and living in the South, or West.

If you were male, you'd have it made in the mate department. No matter where you lived or how old you were. Because women outnumber men, and outlive them.

So the odds aren't good. Now where's the best place to live for a single woman?

According to one poll, Milwaukee, Wisconsin. If you want to be safe, that is. For leadership potential, try our nation's capital, Washington, D.C. That or any of the major cities in California. Looking to get promoted because of your talent? Minneapolis would be your best bet. And you can't beat Seattle for best laws against discrimination. Like Baltimore, Seattle is in a state that has an equal rights amendment.

But if you're looking to get married, follow Horace Greeley's advice: go West. Or South. San Diego is the best place to find single men, having an average of 75 men to every 100 women. Houston comes in second with 74 men to every 100 women. Surprisingly, San Francisco is third, New Orleans fourth and Los Angeles fifth. It seems that where the sun is that's where the jobs are. And where the jobs are, there go the men.

Where the jobs aren't, marriage prospects also aren't as good. Long Island, New York, is the worst for eligible bachelors, having only 49 men per 100 women. Pittsburgh is also the pits, with a mere 52 men for every 100 women. Other areas to move from include Columbus (OH), Buffalo (NY), St. Louis, and Indianapolis. Seems weather isn't the only reason to leave these cities.

Of course, marriage-minded men can expect to do best in exactly those cities where women have the worst odds.

Surprisingly, the total number of unmarried men between sixteen and sixty-four is very nearly equal to the number of unmarried women. Part of the man shortage for older women can be explained by the surplus of men to women that occurs for those twenty-five and younger.

The U.S. Census taken in 1980 shows that the only good time for women to find husbands is between the ages of twenty and twenty-four. At that age, men outnumber women 126 to 100. After that, the odds drop. There are only 77 men for every 100 women aged twenty-five to twenty-nine. Between thirty and thirty-four, women outnumber men 100 to 62. Then it falls off dramatically. For every 100 eligible women aged thirty-five to thirty-nine, there are only 48 unmarried men. Only 38 men to every 100 single women forty-five to forty-nine. And if you're sixty to sixty-four, the odds are definitely not in your favor: there are a mere 27 men to every 100 women.

This isn't helped by the fact that men tend to marry women younger than themselves. And the older the man, the bigger the difference in age between himself and his bride.

Older women are also hurt by the fact that women outlive men. This is changing, with more women entering the workforce and developing the same stress-related life-threatening diseases as men. But it's not changing very quickly. And a large number of unmarried older men are single because they're gay, confirmed bachelors, or have emotional or physical problems that keep them from making a marriage commitment.

Social class is another factor that affects women's marriage possibilities. It's hard for women to marry into a very different social class. For a long time, women have been taught not to marry down. And it's not as easy as the romance novels make out to marry up.

Many a woman has been taught to only consider marrying a man who earns more money than she does. And many a man is threatened by a woman who has a higher salary than he does. So, as women make more money in their careers, their prospects diminish. Education is also a factor that changes the number of men available to a woman. Women tend to marry men at a level of education equal to or above their own.

The only good news, it seems, is that studies show that women are happiest when single. So don't necessarily envy your married sisters. They've got more emotional problems being married than you do being alone. That may be why divorce is so heavily on the upswing. As more and more people realize that marriage isn't the answer all the books and our parents promised it would be.

This fear of divorce, fear of failing may be another factor that contributes to women being single. If marriage is more of a risk, maybe it's not a risk worth taking.

Of course, the fear of being alone generally outweighs the fear of failure. And it keeps women trying to find Mr. Right, wherever they live. All we can say is good luck. And happy hunting.

TEN BEST PLACES TO MEET MEN

1. *Hardware stores.* It may not sound glamorous, but hanging out amidst the nuts and bolts on a Saturday afternoon guarantees that you will be rubbing shoulders with a wide assortment of men.

2. *Lectures.* Go early and scout. Do not be afraid to take a seat next to a likely candidate.

3. *Tennis courts.* This is the best place to show off your legs. Head there on weekends and evenings and hit a ball against the backboard; you will be a good choice if someone needs a partner.

4. *Grocery store.* We all have to eat, so make your chore a "twofer" and do a little man-shopping while you are at it.

5. *Jogging path.* There is no better way to literally run into a dream man. But give it more than a day or two and slowly a natural comraderie will develop among "regulars."

6. *Business district restaurant.* Eating out? Depart from your usual salad bars restaurant and place your order at a steak house in the heart of the financial district.

7. *Commuter train.* Be an early bird and take a seat next to an executive on his way to work before he's frazzled by the day.

8. *Art galleries and museums.* Gazing at famous etchings is a creative way to run into someone special. Be sure to get on your favorite gallery's and museum's mailing list for openings and parties.

9. *Construction site.* Do not think that construction workers are all brawn and no brains. Plenty of them have college degrees along with an unabashed appreciation of women.

10. *Race track.* The best place of all to pick up a winner! The contagious excitement is enough to get any conversation rolling.

TEN BEST PLACES TO MEET WOMEN

1. *Department stores.* Most women love to shop and if you're comfortable initiating a conversation, you can meet lots of fascinating women. Since there are so many types of department stores catering to different women, determine what kind of woman you want to meet, and then go to that store.

2. *Aerobic classes.* Women outnumber men at co-ed health clubs so the odds are in your favor. Just don't forget that most women go to workout classes to exercise, not meet men. However, regardless of the shape you're in, you can meet the kind of women who want to stay in good shape.

3. *Singles lectures.* Women vastly outnumber men at almost all singles classes. Try to attend those seminars that interest you for reasons other than meeting women.

4. *Grocery store.* It's not that women necessarily enjoy cooking more than men, but women don't eat out as much as men. Therefore, head to your nearest market with the kind of questions in mind that women would feel comfortable answering for you. Hint: Ask her opinion about choosing the right seasonings, sauces or vegetables.

5. *Business district restaurant.* If all the faces at your local luncheon eating places are too familiar, try exploring other areas. Where possible, hope for a nice day and look for women eating alone outside.

6. *Art galleries and museums.* What could be easier than casually strolling up to an interesting looking woman and engaging her in conversation about how a particular objet d'art strikes her. There's so much you can talk about. And, when you keep your first few moments of talk focused on what you're looking at, you stand a much greater chance of sitting down for coffee or drinks and talking about yourselves soon after.

7. *Adult education classes.* Find a subject you want to learn more about and that lasts only one or two evenings, then find a seat next to someone who looks interesting. Do remember, however, that not everyone at these classes is single. So, caveat "dater."

8. *Malls.* Like department stores, malls are crowded with women everywhere. Ask their opinion about buying a gift for some female relative.

9. *Athletic events.* More and more women are going in pairs or trios to college or professional sporting

games. What a great way to show your spirit. You can even buy each other a beer or hot dog. Sometimes, it's even easier to meet someone who is rooting for the opposite team!

10. *Parks.* There are lots of women who go to the park to walk their dogs. So long as her animal doesn't take an immediate dislike to you, you have a great chance to meet her. Bring some dog biscuits!

WHERE THE ACTION IS

If you're a newcomer to town you may have trouble finding out where to make connections. Natives know where to go, but how can a newcomer find out where the action is? Local visitors' bureaus and chambers of commerce will not be of much help; their suggestions are often too vague.

We suggest that you pick up a local magazine. These publications usually run ads or listings for the "hottest spots in town." Here is a list of a few such magazines in larger cities. Pick one up next time you are in town:

Atlantic City, N.J.	*Atlantic City Magazine*
Boston, Massachusetts	*Boston Mlagazine*
Buffalo, New York	*Belo*
California	*California Magazine*
Charleston, South Carolina	*Charleston Magazine*
Chicago, Illinois	*Chicago Magazine*
Chicago, Illinois	*Avenue M*
Chicago, Illinois	*Chicago Reader*
Cincinnati, Ohio	*Cincinnati Magazine*
Cleveland, Ohio	*Cleveland Magazine*
Dallas, Texas	*D Magazine*
Denver, Colorado	*Denver Magazine*
Denver, Colorado	*Westword*
Detroit, Michigan	*Detroit Monthly*
Houston, Texas	*Houston Magazine*

Jacksonville, Florida	*Jacksonville Magazine*
Shawnee Mission, Kansas	*Kansas City Magazine*
Los Angeles, California	*Los Angeles Magazine*
Los Angeles, California	*LA Weekly*
Los Angeles, California	*LA Reader*
Madison, Wisconsin	*Madison Select*
Miami, Florida	*Miami Magazine*
Miami, Florida	*Miami South Florida*
Minneapolis, Minnesota	*MPLS Magazine, Twin Cities Reader*
Montreal, Quebec, Canada	*Montreal Calendar Magazine*
Nashville, Tennessee	*Nashville!*
New Haven, Connecticut	*New Haven Info Magazine*
New Orleans, Louisiana	*New Orleans Magazine*
New York, New York	*New York Magazine*
New York, New York	*New York Affairs/ Urban America*
New York, New York	*The Village Voice*
Philadelphia, Pennsylvania	*Philadelphia Magazine*
Pittsburgh, Pennsylvania	*Pittsburgh Magazine*
Portland, Oregon	*Wilame He Week News Weekly*
Richmond, Virginia	*Richmond Magazine*
San Diego, California	*The Weekly*
San Diego, California	*The Reader*
Santa Barbara, California	*Santa Barbara Magazine*
San Francisco, California	*San Francisco Magazine*
San Francisco, California	*The Bay Guardian*

St. Louis, Mo.	*River Front Times*
Tulsa, Oklahoma	*Tulsa Magazine*
Tucson, Arizona	*Tucson Magazine*
Vancouver, B.C., Canada	*Vancouver Magazine*
Washington, D.C.	*Washington Magazine*
Witchita, Kansas	*Wichita Magazine*
Seattle, Washington	*Seattle Business Magazine*
Spokane, Washington	*Spokane Magazine*
Texas	*Texas Monthly*
Toronto	*Saturday Night*
Toronto	*Toronto Life*

How To Meet People

HEALTH CLUBS

Since physical attractiveness is such a big factor in the success of romantic introductions, single people are more likely than marrieds to keep themselves in shape. Any visit to a local health club will probably turn up plenty of singles. So, many health clubs have become meeting grounds for singles that some people have called them "The Singles Bars of the 80s."

Meeting someone this way is not cheap. First of all, there is the membership fee itself. The trend now includes a fat initiation fee, as well as monthly payments; plus, there is the cost of work-out clothes and exercise gear.

For serious minded exercisers, health clubs can be a problem. There are plenty of single women who come dressed to "the nines" including a strong perfume, which can sometimes make for a rather strange aromatic environment. Also, there can be so much socializing going on that access to pieces of exercise equipment can be difficult.

Aerobics or Jazzercise-type classes can provide a great way to stay in shape, as well as meet people. There's no doubt about the attraction of seeing healthy, pulsating bodies in often skin-tight attire moving to the sounds of disco music.

Two other ways to make the club work for you is to lounge around the snack bar or lobby. You'll soon begin to see familiar faces, making introductions that much easier. You may also find some of the club's tournaments or activities a way to meet new people.

Unfortunately, many singles who have less than beautiful physiques feel quite intimidated by those who are already in shape. Older singles also feel a little out of place by the mostly younger clientele.

PERSONAL ADS

Personal ads have been around a lot longer than most people think. How do you think so many of the lonely men who pioneered the opening of the Old West found wives? They advertised in big city newspapers (hence the term mail-order brides). Personal ads have always flourished when social connections break down, and it is not much different today.

Romance in the want ads has always attracted a curious audience. Many who claimed they would never place or answer an ad have nevertheless grown somewhat addicted to the soap opera quality of others' romantic cravings.

Personals were once associated with people seeking alternative sex styles or those desperate for a date or mate, but now have become a happy hunting ground for many singles. Almost every major city magazine or urban alternative newspaper has a section devoted to them. This growing trend has not only made money for these media, but has also given rise to several books and numerous

39

seminars. The personals still attract very different people; from the serious and genuinely single desirous of a real relationship, to married executives desiring extramarital affairs, to lonely prisoners in search of pen pals.

There are many benefits to using the personals:

1. If you like to receive a lot of mail, you stand a good chance of getting just what you want (provided what you say about yourself is intriguing enough).
2. The anonymity of not revealing who you are, yet still piquing interest among members of the opposite sex, can be enjoyable.
3. It doesn't cost much—particularly if you are the responder, rather than the advertiser.
4. The opportunity to meet educated singles who are drawn by the power of the written word.

A few of the major disadvantages are that people frequently misrepresent who they really are, particularly about their looks. They figure that once you meet them you won't mind the differences. And there is no way to ensure that everyone who advertises or responds is single.

How to write your personal ad. Before placing your ad, consider what kind of people you want to meet and select an appropriate publication. Different people read *Screw Magazine* than read *The New York Review of Books.*

Understand the special language of personals. Abbreviations that are most commonly used are:

M	Married
S	Single
D	Divorced
M	Male
F	Female
YO	Years old
W	White
B	Black
J	Jewish
P/P	Photo/phone

PIX	Send photo
SASE	Self-addressed stamped envelope
ISO	In search of

Some other issues to remember when writing an ad include the following:

1. Give details about yourself that you would want to know about others (height, age, race, weight). Be honest or you'll find yourself on the receiving end of a very harsh reaction.
2. List your interests, but try not to come across as too involved in them. Otherwise, you might give the impression that you don't have the time for anyone new in your life, or that a new friend must also share your interest.
3. Be specific about what kind of relationship you are looking for.
4. Don't be afraid to express something that is really important to you.
5. Inject some humor into your ad. Who doesn't appreciate a good laugh?
6. When responding, make certain that you choose fine stationery. Write, print or type neatly and try to avoid cross-outs, misspellings, and grammatical mistakes.
7. When sending a photograph, send the best one you have. Looks are important to people. Above all, don't send a photo that includes anyone of the opposite sex with you; it might appear to be your former mate!
8. Don't be afraid to experiment with different ads about yourself. Even if you don't get precisely the response you are looking for, you will be certain to learn a lot more about yourself from describing yourself.
9. When you receive a response, write or call immediately! This person wants to meet you! Also, the longer you wait, the greater the chances are that this person has already met someone else, or has forgotten about you.

SINGLES ACTIVITIES CLUBS

No matter where you live, you can find a singles group to suit your needs. There are so many such groups that often newspapers dedicate weekly columns to listing their activities. These organizations range from well established national ones such as Parents Without Partners to small groups of unmarried animal lovers, hikers, square dancers, geniuses, motorcycle riders, and non-smokers. In San Francisco, for example, there are even clubs for singles who speak foreign languages and who hold advanced educational degrees. Yearly dues can be as little as a few dollars or as much as several hundred. But whatever kind of club you choose will let you socialize selectively with others in a non-pressured environment. You will have an opportunity to establish lasting relationships with members of both sexes, something not guaranteed by the casual encounters of workshops and bars. Consider the following things while scouting for or participating in a singles club:

Make sure the group is well organized. Since singles are often transient or do not stay single forever, clubs without strong leadership have a tendency to fizzle.

Ask a friend to join with you. It can be difficult to face several pairs of strange eyes without some support.

If heavy membership fees are involved, ask to attend a meeting or activity so you can question members at random about whether it is worth the price.

Do not judge a group by one activity. If fees are not an issue, go a couple of times to give it a fair chance. If that club really does not suit your needs, try another.

Get actively involved. Volunteer for a committee rather than restricting participation to an occasional social function. You will get to know people better and probably enjoy yourself more.

Join more than one club. You will broaden your circle of friends while filling your social calendar.

Start your own club. Put up notices at your apartment complex, church, the health club and in your community newspaper to advertise for members and people who might want to be organizers.

VIDEO DATING

I met my wife, Stephanie, through video dating. The odds of our finding each other through friends or chance encounter were virtually non-existent; we didn't work, play or shop in the same neighborhood.

It wasn't love at first sight. I was convinced that "love started at 5'5" (I'm 6'2"), and she was only 5'1". As physically breath-taking as she was, I never would have stopped long enough to get to know her. Fortunately, I had the opportunity to find out more about her by watching her videotape. It was only then that I realized how truly lovely and fascinating she was.

That's a big plus about video dating: you can spot someone intriguing yet not feel pressured to make up your mind immediately as to whether or not to make the first move. Although we met in the office of Great Expectations, most people meet when they read a written profile and see a few photographs about each other. Then, they watch a five to eight minute color videotape. By this time, they have really gotten insights into someone's personality, character, and of course, physical qualities. Chemistry between the viewer and the on-screen Member can be electrifying.

Each Member has the privilege of selecting any other Member. Once chosen, it is up to the chosen Member to respond "yes" or "no." Only when there is mutual consent are full names and telephone numbers exchanged. It's confidential, discreet and allows both Members to be in full control about who they will meet. It's also enormously time-saving because you only go out with someone whom you want to meet, and who wants to meet you. Once both

Members have consented to meet, they are given each other's phone numbers and are free to call one another.

Their first date is so much more like their second because they have both pre-screened each other with no middleman. Usually, they meet for a bite to eat or for drinks. Instead of the usual "interview" that accompanies the awkwardness of the first date, Members already know about each other's lifestyle, occupation, hobbies, activities and what qualities they are looking for in someone of the opposite sex. As a result, the first date is more comfortable and exciting.

Since Americans are so visually-oriented, video dating is a natural for singles interested in dating someone who is physically appealing. But unlike chance encounters, which rely almost totally on immediate physical attractiveness, video dating allows Members to sit back and take their time learning about each other. Therefore, as potent as the physical screening is, it is only one of several screening tools.

Many Members of video dating services are attracted by the video screening benefits. However, some companies provide additional services, such as parties and seminars. The largest and oldest one, Great Expectations, offers its Membership unique opportunities to meet other Members in the same city or across the country who share similar special interests, hobbies, business pursuits or traveling agendas. Sporting, cultural and travel activities are also offered nearly every week.

RADIO DATING

Radio dating? It's worked for some. Hotlines around the country are taking names and numbers of interested singles and making them available to (hopefully compatible) others. Brief profiles are given over the air by momentary celebrities who broadcast their age, interests, and romantic aspirations for all to hear.

WRKO in Boston, a pace setter in this field, has received both publicity and good results. A few weddings have resulted from meetings via this medium, and more than a few relationships have flourished. Most of the callers on this show and others like it are people who shun dating services and singles bars. Initial contacts through radio dating are telephone calls that offer revelation while diminishing the risks of face-to-face encounters. "Clients" of this method report their contacts to be primarily nice and interesting people, with an occasional pest or obscene caller. Out of this response, many find one or two respondents with whom they become friends, and if they are lucky, serious lovers.

The concept of radio dating was created by Dick Syatt, WRKO's hotline host. He initiated the idea in Dallas in 1976, then established the format in Providence, Rhode Island. Other stations around the country have followed suit, indicating that this is not a flash-in-the-pan fad, but rather a viable and increasingly acceptable way for singles ot meet.

SELF-HELP WORKSHOPS

Scan the newspaper or browse through a college catalog and you will stumble across them in droves—the self-help workshops. Because they cater to singles, one newspaper tagged them the "singles bars of the 80s." Common workshop topics include coping with divorce, learning to be assertive, understanding sexuality, or improving love relationships. They are usually offered by colleges and counseling centers, but some are promoted by people who simply rent office space for an evening or weekend. Fees range anywhere from two dollars to thirty dollars and up.

Many of these seminars claim to offer holistic ways of spiritual healing while increasing self-actualization. They attempt to accomplish those goals through various methods, including games, relaxation techniques, intimate group discussions, lectures, and one-to-one exercises. Although such workshops have enjoyed sustained popularity for several years, they do not have the blessing of the psychiatric community. One New York psychiatry professor branded leaders of such seminars "quadrophonic Freuds" who exploit the isolation of others.

It is probably true that whatever information someone can impart to you on a Saturday morning could probably be discovered through a pop psychology magazine or on a television talk show. But it is doubtful anyone takes such workshops seriously since few who attend are really in need of professional help. Instead, workshops are beneficial in simply bringing together people who share a common problem. They can also provide an avenue for recently separated, widowed, or divorced people to get back in circulation.

The best advice for approaching a self-help workshop is to go with an open mind and without expecting to discover a new you and the partner of your dreams in one evening. Other things to consider include:

Check the credentials of whomever is conducting the workshop. Although some may have training as psychologists, counselors, and social workers, many are businessmen and teachers who probably are not any more qualified to address a particular topic than you would be.

Be prepared to let your hair down. As stated earlier, some leaders will require you to participate in games and exercises. One leader of an ongoing seminar in Southern California likes to get things rolling by having workshop participants stroll around the room as if they were on a ship deck.

Don't expect to meet droves of dateable people. This holds true particularly for women since they tend to outnumber men. Participants also tend to be in the over-thirty-five crowd.

Be aware that seminars conducted by counseling centers may simply be giveaways to promote more expensive services such as one-to-one therapy.

Do not feel pressured into having to meet anyone. Some workshops turn into free-for-alls when several women try to hustle the one attractive man in the room during the coffee break.

Even if you do not meet someone special at one of these workshops, you still might receive some valuable knowledge about yourself.

BARWASH

Yes, you read correctly; Barwash. Those of you who live around Austin, Texas, have an opportunity to turn doing laundry into a social outing.

Rob Walsh was weary of spending time in dull, dingy laundromats. So he opened his own place and created an environment to add some sparkle to a mundane but necessary task.

Barwash is all glass and wicker and spotless blue and white tiles. There's deli food available as well as beer. A glass wall divides the laundromat from the restaurant and bar so as to assure a serene social environment. Whether or not this is the place for you to meet Mr. or Ms. Right I really can't say. But, if you have a load of dirty laundry, a handful of quarters and live in or around Austin it certainly is worth a shot. The rest of us will have to wait until Walsh makes good on his promise to franchise his operation.

Nice Girls Do Pick Up Men!

The term "pick up" has dubious connotations, but all it really means is starting a conversation with or sharing the company of another person casually and informally. Women have been picking up men—and making it easy for men to pick them up— for a long time, and in the 1980s, it is worth a woman's effort to try it once or twice.

If you've a woman, just how do you go about this? Let yourself meet someone in a public place, at the supermarket, for example. What about the man who is grumbling at the line for the deli counter? Answer his grumbles with something that invites further conversation, such as, "I've been living here for two years but I never came into this store before. I'm shocked to see such a crowd." His reaction will tell you if he is a crazy person who talks to himself, if he is still annoyed and does not want to talk to you, or if he suddenly is glad to be stuck on line with an attractive and talkative woman.

Say that you have somehow gotten into a conversation with a man, the vibes are good, but you are late for an appointment or a bus. Be sure to ask the person his name; that way you can tell him yours. If you have business cards, why not offer him one when you say goodbye? It is safe for both of you; you are not giving away personal information about where you live, and he may find it easier to call you at work where he knows the call will be kept short. If you do not have cards, mention where you work when you tell him your name, and as you leave, suggest that he call you there. You could also tell the person to look you up if you are listed in the phone book, but you may not feel safe doing that. Of course you can always jot your number down and say you would love to talk to him again.

What about men who are casual acquaintances or the men you talk to at parties? Why not, if you find you share interests with someone, suggest that you see a particular movie together? Sometimes you will only have to make the suggestion; if the man is interested, he will immediately try to make the plans definite. Or if the conversation is particularly good, suggest that the two of you have lunch together to continue the discussion; if your new friend is receptive to the idea, set up a specific time to meet.

Just remember that most men are afraid of losing control of a relationship. A woman is taught to be flattered when a man asks her out, and his interest in her is often enough to encourage her to start being interested in him. But some men cannot accept the idea that they have not chosen the woman first and will not respond positively to a woman's first move—unless they do not realize that the woman made the first move. Other men love the attention. And in cases where a woman really just wants to be friends, her staying in touch with the man can become the basis for a fuller relationship later.

Whatever the success rate is of women picking up men, it is a good thing for a woman to try, if only to see for once how a man feels.

And—for once—not to have to *wait* for the phone to ring!

DO'S AND DON'TS OF FIRST DATES

Keep a sense of humor. Be able to laugh—at yourself.

Do ask your date questions about his/her interests, but don't get too personal with questions about income or religion.

Don't ask a friend to call during the evening to see how things are going.

Don't expect perfection. One of you will probably end up with a foot in the mouth or a spilled drink.

Do try to avoid running on at the mouth. Nervousness often causes us to keep talking about trivial or—to be honest—stupid things. Learn to enjoy the tension of anticipation that you feel during a pause in conversation.

Do be sweet and friendly, but try not to get too gushy and romantic too soon. You'll end up scaring the daylights out of your date, and risking never seeing him or her again.

Avoid indulging in too much alcohol because you feel nervous. You'll make a bad impression and may really turn the person off if you throw up all over the car. Also, use of drugs might offend a new acquaintance.

Refrain from telling your date how much he or she reminds you of an old lover. Also avoid details of past affairs. If you find your date attractive and are definitely considering going to bed with him or her, let him know of your desire in gentle, flattering ways. Avoid wrestling holds that leave the other person no way out.

Don't expect sex. Not for any reason. It may happen, and it may not. It must be a mutual choice, not payment for an expensive dinner or the natural conclusion of all contemporary dates.

Don't read from any list of questions that you might prepare for first date. No one likes to be grilled, especially in a presumably romantic setting.

Getting Rid Of First Date Jitters

No matter how popular and self-assured we are, no matter how experienced we may be at dating, first dates often cause apprehension and anxiety. As we get older and more experienced, these jitters are nowhere near as acute as they were during our teens, when zits threw us into tailspins, our palms sweated, and our hair never looked worse no matter how much time and attention we spent on it.

First dates are rarely with people we know well, and when they are, they are usually just casual get-togethers. We may not know our date very well, and we want to make a good impression and show ourselves off to our best advantage. Even if no great romance results from this, at stake tonight is time, effort, money, and the basic human desire to be liked and accepted. We may also be hoping, openly or secretly, that a good, stable, loving relationship evolves from this evening.

The advice we were given when we first started dating holds just as true today. For a first date, it is often best to plan some activity which will provide a source of conversation and a reduction in tension. Although many couples start with dinner for two, it is often better to go to a show or concert or party so you will not have to force the conversation.

When preparing for a first date, it is always good to allow plenty of time to get ready. A long shower or bath will relax you. Looking your best is important. It will give you self-confidence.

Be sure your clothes are appropriate to the occasion. You will not want to wear a pair of jeans and a T-shirt to an elegant restaurant. If you are not dressed properly, you will end up with an even greater case of the jitters.

When getting ready, allow yourself a few minutes extra to sip a drink, read a book, or just relax before you go.

Just in case you end up in bed that night, wear clean, sexy underwear.

Have with you a small bottle of perfume or men's cologne for touch-ups, a toothbrush, and a small bottle of breath freshener.

Carry birth control with you just in case. Do not spoil an unexpectedly romantic encounter because you forgot these essentials.

In case you both end up at your house for an evening of romance, keep an extra toothbrush or two handy. You might also want to keep an extra one-size-fits-all terry robe around for quick dashes to the bathroom or for after the shower.

Have scented candles and some wine in preparation for a romantic interlude.

Each first date is a journey into the unknown. This may be a one-time-only experience, or the start of something wonderful. Either way, there's no accurate way to predict the outcome, so just relax and enjoy yourself.

What Not To Say

No matter how hard we try to avoid catastrophe, there inevitably comes the time when, in searching for just the right thing to say to someone new, our foot ends up in our mouth.

The setting is simple and idyllic: a special person invites you over for a romantic dinner for two, unveils a beautiful nouvelle cuisine setting and, in an effort to be modest, says, "I hope you like all this stuff." And in your eagerness to be reassuring, you blurt out, "Oh, sure, I ate this kind of food last night!" Thus does your eagerly awaited Night of a Thousand Delights quickly become the Night of the Living Dead.

Relax. There are ways to rekindle the flames of passion even after your mouth has performed like a fire extinguisher.

Ways to treat foot-in-mouth disease. The biggest mistake most people make after a blooper is becoming consumed by their own embarrassment and ignoring the other person's feelings. If your faux pas has hurt his or her feelings, your mission is to make reparations. Here are some ideas.

Touch the person immediately in a gentle, caring way. Your words may have caused a temporary rift, and reestablishing contact immediately with a touch can be worth a thousand words.

Admit your mistake and take back what you said with appropriate apologies and explanations. But do not overdo it. Let the length of the apology fit the seriousness of the goof.

Try to find an explanation. If you think fast and perform convincingly, you might be able to reverse the entire situation: "I was only talking about these great potatoes, which my mother tried to make for the first time last night, but they didn't turn out well. I'll have to tell her how you did it!"

Keep your sense of humor. Even if you have no way of retracting the statement, your friendly touch and embarrassed laugh can make the other person feel he is sharing an intimate moment with you. But: if you actually laugh, be sure the person knows you are laughing at yourself.

Use the situation to your advantage by saying, "I've goofed enough for one night. The next silly remark is up to you."

When you make a mistake, the other person sees you with your defenses down; that is why it is a potentially intimate situation. Our imperfections make us human; those of us who try to be perfect come across as boring and phony. Chances are that if you admit your mistake, you will give the other person an opportunity to unmask a bit, too.

Topics to avoid. The entire subject of your "ex" is a swamp where a budding relationship can sink. It may be the first thing on your mind, but it's probably the last thing that the other person wants to hear. Do not make comparisons between a new friend and previous lovers or dates. New relationships should be developed with fresh insights, not emotional leftovers from others. Make the person feel unique, not typecast.

Stay away from downbeat subjects like your recent depression, physical infirmities, limitations, handicaps, or deformities until a comfortable point later in the relationship. It's still a good idea to avoid politics and religion until you have some idea of how and when they may be dis-cussed without worsening the world situation. And in general, avoid making sweeping pronouncements on any sensitive subject such as sex, marriage, or money until you get an indication of their point of view. At all times, make the effort to tune in to the other person's reactions. There may be some areas that are comfortable to you but strange or painful to them. Stay alert and tread softly.

Saying No

BREAKING DATES

The breaking of a date is not that serious and can vary ac-cording to the degrees of breakage. First degree breaks are those that deal with either side not wanting to have the date and calling to make note of that.

"Look, I don't want to go out with you tonight."

"You could have at least called me sooner. I mean, it's five minutes to seven, and our date is for seven-thirty. What kind of decency is that?"

First degree has double-edged honesty, and if it happens on the first few dates, without compassion and under-standing for the person the date is being broken with, it could be the line that breaks up the relationship.

Second degree breakage is caused by something that happens internally or externally to the person doing the breaking. "I am not in the habit of breaking dates twenty minutes before it's time to go out, but I thought I would be feeling better by this evening, but I am not."

You're stuck for a moment, but at least the message seemed honest, until she calls out to someone knocking at the door, "Wait a minute, I can't get the door yet. I am still on the phone."

Third degree breaks have to do with the unexpected. Someone came in from out of town, an emergency in the family, an ex-boyfriend or girlfriend needs a short shot of emotional therapy. The best way to deal with this situation, if you want to see the person again, is to tell them the reason and then immediately offer another invitation for a date soon.

Fourth degree date breaking concerns people who do not make dates with people they do not want to go out with. They do not make dates without considering seriously if they do or do not want to go out with anyone. Fourth degree civility concerns itself with not allowing yourself to make the wrong choice.

"Sarah, would you like to go out with me on Friday?"

"No, I can't make it on Friday."

"What about Saturday, then?"

"Saturday night I can't make it either. I've got a lot of work to do this next week."

"What about the following weekend or some night during the week?"

"No, I am busy all during the week and on the weekend nights, too."

"What about next month?"

"No, next month isn't good, either. I've got a lot of things to do, and I seem to be tied up with everybody."

"No time for me, huh; well, what about the following month?"

"No, I don't think so."

"You mean you're going to go on and on without going out with me at all?"

"That's the way it looks right now. If anything changes though I'll certainly let you know."

The fourth degreers are constantly getting applause and praise from those who don't know how to say no, those who spend much of their dating time with everybody but the people they want to go out with.

HOW TO END A DATE EARLY

It would be great if every date (particularly the first date with someone) was enjoyed by both people. To adapt a show business phrase: "Leave then wanting more."

But, what happens if one or both people want to call it quits early? How do you extricate yourself without insulting the other person?

HERE ARE A FEW TIPS:

"Gee (His or her first name), I've got to get up early tomorrow morning. I guess we should call it a night." Say what you have to get up to do, if you like.

"(His or her name), I think that you're a fine person, but you're not my type. I think you should take me back to my house." (Or, "I think I should take you back to your house."

"(His or her name), I don't feel very well. I guess it was something that I ate. I want to go home."

After you make a phone call, you say: "I just called my office (or my babysitter), and I've got to go to my office (or home) now."

HOW TO DISCOURAGE A SUITOR

1. Don't listen. When the person realizes how disinterested you are, chances are he or she will leave you alone.
2. Don't make eye contact.
3. Refuse all offers to get together (dates, dances, drinks, invitations to conversation about any subject).
4. Be unavailable for any contact.
5. Find out what the person likes or wants and do the opposite.

6. Be in a hurry.
7. Do not praise, congratulate, or be positive about the other person.
8. Be overly critical.
9. Discuss subjects that are "turn offs" to him or her.
10. Be honest and straightforward. Tell the person that you don't wish to date or develop any further relationship with him or her under any circumstances.

The Opening Lines

During encounters with the opposite sex, you've undoubtedly had occasion to exclaim, "Boy! What a line!" But have you ever paused to define exactly what a line is? It will meet three criteria:

First, it will be recited with an ulterior motive; *second,* it will sound somewhat rehearsed or cliched ("We could make such beautiful music together..."); and *third,* it won't be sincere.

The only rule about opening lines is that they should at least be appropriate to the circumstances. It's better to say "May I share your umbrella" if you are caught in a sudden downpour than if you are at Malibu Beach in August, but even in the latter case that line can work if delivered with humor. If you are shy, then say something you are comfortable with, and not something you remember from an old Bogart and Bacall movie.

More important is the dialogue that goes on after you've met someone.

What is your impression of the other person? Do you

think he or she would appreciate humor, kindness, or boldness? Remember that the sincerity of your desire to make contact sends the ball into the other person's court, and that is all an opening line can ever do. Remember that women as well as men need to think about opening lines.

WHAT TO SAY

"Hello!" As obvious as it may seem, the most successful opening line is "Hello!" This lovely word has several advantages: it is direct, friendly, and easy to pronounce. If delivered with a smile, it will almost always beget a smile and thus start things off on the right foot. It also allows you to induce the essential eye contact that will tell you what to do next. Its only potential drawback is that it does not necessarily open up a topic of conversation, but it is guaranteed to make anyone short of a Grinch feel good and want to talk back.

Compliments. Like a warm "Hello!", a nice compliment will bring out almost anyone's sunny side. But remember, a compliment must be sincere, specific, and not too personal. These are good: "I like your necklace"; "That's a very pretty scarf."

This is not: "You've got a great ass!" That one could quickly lead to the bedroom or the first-aid cabinet. Use only if prepared for the consequences.

Questions. Any kind of question can get you into a conversation, but the best questions are those that reflect a specific awareness of the other person. And, if you are comfortable being just a bit coy, it is not even necessary to ask something you really want to know. But it is best if you ask something that you think the other person will be happy to answer.

Thus,

"Are you interested in James Joyce, too?" is good to ask of someone who is holding a copy of *Ulysses.*

"Do you know which of these wines would go best with veal?" is not bad for that attractive person you spot at the liquor store.

Questions that are too general or too serious should be avoided. You can always ask what your new friend thinks of the economy on the *second* date.

Cliches. There is no need to avoid cliche lines. The reason they are used so often is that they work so well. Take into account that they are cliches and say them with appropriate humor, or make your own variations of them.

"Haven't we met somewhere before?" is the oldest one in the book, but it remains a charming excuse to strike up a conversation. Besides, sometimes people do see people they think they met before.

"What's a nice girl like you doing in a place like this?" The idea behind that line is, "You seem to be different from most of the people here. Are you new to this place?" So be creative with it and use it in a way that suits the circumstances.

Seeking or offering assistance. Every human being wants to feel like he or she makes a difference, a great way to open a conversation is to ask for or offer help. Just keep your eyes open and be inventive.

"Can I hold that package for you?"

"Pardon me, could you reach that for me, please?" or "Let me reach that for you."

"This is my first time in this store. Do you know where they keep the electrical equipment?"

Clever lines. If being clever (and usually forward, too) appeals to you, and you think such a tactic would work with the other person, you might try virtually anything that comes to mind:

"Wasn't I married to you once before?"

"Is it true that beautiful women/men are generally friendly to strangers?"

"I'll bet you a lunch that I can get you to go to lunch with me."

Being honest. Lastly, because no matter what you choose to say, your meaning is "I want to meet you," you might try being open about it and simply saying:

"I don't mean to be too forward, but I simply can't resist trying to meet you!"

"You have a very interesting face."

"Hi, I'm Jeffrey. Who are you?"

All of these opening lines are mere suggestions. Adopt or adapt them to your specific situation and your own personality; invent better ones. While the meaning behind the words never varies, a successful opening line is one that reflects the real you. Some kinds of lines typical to new relationships are discussed below.

Opening lines. As noted earlier, opening lines are used as a pretext to initiate a possible relationship. Rather than directly expressing our interest in a stranger whose reaction might then be equally direct and painful, we give a line which hints at what we want, leaving both people an easy out of the situation.

"Haven't we met somewhere before?" ("I want to meet you.")

"I doubt it, unless you've lived in Reykjavik, Iceland." ("I don't want to meet you.")

This response could even be taken as a "yes" if delivered in a certain tone, but the point is that any deception in an opening line is generally obvious and therefore harmless. Like every aspect of communication, lines become more complicated and potentially dangerous as the relationship deepens.

Bedtime stories. The first juncture in a relationship where lines become a significant cause for misunderstanding comes at the "to bed or not to bed" stage. Lines can be put to good use here when they soften the hurt of rejection ("I'm already involved" rather than "Not even if it would clear up the national debt"), but they can lead to problems, too. Especially the first time, two partners can have very different needs and expectations about the sexual act, and this leaves great room for emotional manipulation via a good line or two. In fact, sometimes it's nearly impossible to resist.

"Nobody has ever turned me on like this before."

"Of course I really love you!"

"I want something more from you than just sex."

"I want you spiritually *and* physically!"

"This is not going to be just a one-night stand."

"I'm just not ready to get physical yet."

"Let's wait until we know each other better."

"What's the hurry? We've got the rest of our lives."

How to interpret a line. The difficulty in providing insightful commentary on lines like these is that no one but the people involved can know the degree of truth expressed. What sounds like a well rehearsed seduction line may well be meant entirely in earnest by someone who just doesn't know how to put it any better. As, for example, the following exchanges.

"I think I'm falling in love with you already!"

Motive #1. He or she really means this. Will such heartfelt sincerity be recognized? Stay tuned!

Response #1. "Did you really expect me to be stupid enough to fall for that old line?" Whoops! Another beautiful romance falls victim to cynicism.

"I think I'm falling in love with you already!"

Motive #2. Beware! He or she is out for a one-night stand while his/her real lover is away for the weekend.

Response #2. "Oh, God, how beautiful! I feel the same way!" And yet another of love's fools takes an unwitting plunge off the Cliffs of Despair into the Valley of Tears.

It is an unfortunate fact of human nature that our search for love may blindly lead us first to Response #2 and then, by protective reaction, to Response #1, regardless of the other person's sincerity. Once burned, ever cautious, they say, a problem as old as love itself, and not even this book can pretend to solve that one. We all share the same tendency to listen with our hearts rather than our ears, and so long as we are able to love, we are capable of being manipulated by it. But let's not give up on love! The only advice here is to consider the person behind the line rather than the line itself and remember that even the smartest fish may at some point be snared by the cheapest lure.

Some other lines you may hear.

"Call me next week."
"I'll call you."
"I didn't have time to call you."
"You never call me."
"I called you, but the line was busy."
"Maybe I wrote down your number wrong. Is
    it...?"
"Some other time, perhaps."
"Can't we be just friends?"
"I'll go crazy trying to think of you as just a
    friend."
"I'm your friend. I'll never hurt you."
"I'm getting back together with my boyfriend (or
    girlfriend)."
"I like you, but I need my space right now."
"You're a wonderful person."
"I just can't get into romantic hassles right now."

"I'm afraid of getting too involved."
"I don't think I'm right for you."
"It's not you, it's me."
"You won't let me down, will you?"
"You're the best I've ever had!'

Fishing Lines

This is the kind of line one uses when casting about for some kind of reassurance, like a compliment, a kiss, a warm touch or a soothing word. This line will never openly admit exactly what the person wants, but a sensitive listener should have no trouble tuning in, if only to the fact that there's more there than meets the ear.

"I'll bet you didn't think of me even once all day."
"Does this bikini fit okay?" (When she knows damn
     well it does!)
"I look just awful."
"Nobody likes me any more."

Lines such as these are used to test the temperature of the relationship at the exact moment. Is the other person concerned and responsive? And, if the line does not provoke the desired response (as, for example, "Nobody likes me any more," calls for something like, "Oh, don't feel bad. I love you."), the next step is usually, "You never listen to what I say, you *#!!%#!" Which brings us to...

Salvation Lines

Salvation Lines may be used in a variety of situations, all of which may be lumped together under the general heading of "Extracting Feet From Mouth and Relationship From Deep Freeze." Perhaps you were juggling two relationships at once and couldn't remember what you said to whom. Perhaps you used your ex's name on your current love. (Also known in dating as Instant Ouch.) Perhaps you want the relationship one way and he/she wants it another, so your lines had better be chosen very carefully. Perhaps you were simply insensitive without intending to be. In any case, it is a good idea to have some soothing and smoothing First Aid Lines ready just in case.

"I didn't mean to call you that name. That's my brother's/sister's name. I can't believe I said that. You don't remind me of him/her at all!" (And you might throw in a few "Wow!"'s for good effect, too.)

"I only called you by his/her name because it was on my mind. He/she tried to call me today, but I wouldn't come to the phone." (NOTE: This Salvation Line for Instant Ouch comes with no money-back guarantee. If you can patent a foolproof one, you will die rich.)

"I know why I thought you were at that movie with me. It's because I wanted to take you but you were busy that night, so I went with my sister/brother/cousin/ aged aunt instead."

"I'm sorry I wasn't listening. I had just an incredibly depressing day at work, and it's hard to get my mind off it. Sit in my lap and tell me again."

"I did notice how good you looked! I just didn't say it out loud. I whistled under my breath."

Obviously, it can be a blessing to come from a family with several brothers and sisters. If you have none, don't despair. Use cousins, then try platonic or gay friends (preferably neutered-looking or remarkably unattractive ones). Or, if you must, invent any or all of the above, but please be consistent. In any case, if your genuine intent is to comfort the other person, you will stand a good chance of selling the Salvation Line, at least for the time being.

It is a good idea to avoid some of these complications in the first place by making a conscious effort to separate relationships in your mind. Don't allow yourself to become confused by any similarities between your ex and your present. If you are seeing more than one person, make a strenuous mental effort to note where you went and what you said with whom. A clever strategy is to let them do most of the talking when you become unsure of any basic facts (like their name, their address, whether or not you have slept together, etc.) And remember that, when presenting a Salvation Line, your delivery had better be very convincing, because the lines themselves are always a bit hokey. As a final bit of advice, try to make some appropriate physical contact at the same time. At points like this, a little bit of seduction can go a long way.

Stretch Lines

This is a ticklish category, because it involves situations where one or both persons are treading water in the relationship, unsure of which way to swim. You don't want the relationship to go under, but you are not sure you want to be marooned with that person forever, either. So, in effect, you decide not to decide, and you stretch your present situation into the foreseeable future. You stall for time and maintain a certain amount of distance between the partners.

"I care for you very much. I'm just not sure what 'love' is."
"Things are so nice the way they are. Why change them?"
"Let's not rush into anything."
"You're the most important person in my life today, but I don't want to predict what may happen tomorrow."
"I don't want to mislead you."
"Parts of me just refuse to be tied down to one person."
"I just don't want you to be hurt by liking me too much."
"You don't know me like you think you know me."

There is a fine line between Stretch Lines and Exit Lines and, in fact, some lines cross the line and serve both categories, depending on the user's intent or the listener's inference.

Exit Lines

When one person has to end it all, a line, devious as it may seem, is often the best way, provided that it does not betray any trust or confidences built up during the course of a relationship. You don't blithely tell a person to shove off with, "All's fair in love and war" unless you enjoy being suicidal or sadistic. However, the right line can sum things up in a gentle and wistfully romantic way that leaves a feeling of "Tis far better to have loved and lost...", and provides a buoyant spirit rather than a sinking one.

"I'll always be better for having known you."
"You're a wonderful man/woman and will make some lucky person very happy some day."
"This is just the way it had to be for us both."
"I'm most concerned that you don't take this the wrong way."
"We'll always have Paris." (or Poughkeepsie or Lompoc or...)
"Here's looking at you, kid."

You get the idea. Sometimes it's best to ride a well-shod old horse over a well-trod old path, recognizing that, no matter how unique your own emotional journey may seem to you, it is most likely both a familiar and a fabled one for mankind. So, when you look behind the line, you may see one person or millions of people who have shared similarly complex feelings and were only able to express them with a few, simple words.

HOW TO INTERPRET A LINE

What you have to learn about lines is how to interpret them correctly, lest you be manipulated by them time and again. Following are some of those well-trod lines and their possible hidden meanings:

"I'm separated." (I haven't seen my spouse since breakfast.)
"I like liberated women." (The bra-less kind who pay their own way.)
"Why isn't a great guy (or girl) like you married?" (What's wrong with you that I don't know about?)
"I've never said this to anyone before." (Not today anyway.)

"I'm not ready for a relationship, yet." (Not with you
at least.)
"I'll still respect you in the morning." (It's the
afternoon you'll have to worry about.)
"Let's play it by ear." (Mine.)
"I promise if I stay over, we'll just cuddle."
(Until I can talk you into something else.)
"I'm the kind of guy who likes a lot of space."
(I don't want this to be a regular thing.)
"I'll call you." (So long.)

But before you throw up your hands in despair at prospects of being caught in a crossfire of insincere prattle,
consider that not all lines are bad. Some bolster egos
while others spare feelings. Few of us could openly turn
down someone we don't want to date, so we substitute
half-truths about being busy or having out-of-town guests.
That way rejection isn't personal.

WHY USE A LINE

Have you ever heard the line, "Don't give me that
line!"? And did you stop to consider the fact that this line
is just another way of saying that someone else's statement resembles a cow pie, which itself is just another way
of saying "bull——," or "I don't believe you"? Sound con-
voluted? Well, nobody ever told you life was going to be
simple, and lines certainly seem to make life more complicated. But they are an important part of the human
game, and it is good to understand their nature and use if
we wish to be better gamesmen/women.

What exactly is a line? Webster may offer seventy-nine
definitions in its unabridged dictionary, but we shall narrow it considerably to "an oft-repeated phrase which con-
tains an element of intended deception and involves an ulterior motive." This may seem to have negative
implications, but let us consider both sides of the coin.

Lines are a bridge between reality and fantasy, a natural part of that wondrous entity called human language

whereby we assign specific words to represent fathomless and amorphous feelings. But let's not get too heady. This only means that we all, to one extent or another, feel one thing and say another, either because we can't find the right word or because we don't want to find the right word. Hence, it is socially convenient to have ready lines to fit every occasion. Lines are also a good way to avoid a head-on collision with some of life's unpleasant realities, such as the pain of rejection and the pain of rejecting others. Just as we have invented soft, cushiony chairs to save our fair skins from sharp rocks and noisome dirt, so we have concocted comforting, fluffy language to protect our equally delicate emotions. So, don't look upon lines as necessarily wrong or hypocritical, but rather as a part of our condition that we can work for good or ill.

As a part of the Singles Culture, it behooves you to be aware of lines—when to use them and when they are being used on you—in order to have a firmer grip on relations with the opposite sex. Lines can be dangerous because they involve a certain amount of deceit which, if mistaken for honesty, can cause hurt and complications. Remember that any line is somewhere between one and one hundred percent bull—and that its purpose may be to cause pain or to protect from pain. In this latter case, a line is also known as a "white lie," but unfortunately, even these have been known to cause their share of misunderstanding and heartache. As they say, "Oh, what a tangled web we weave...."

The object of the Line Game, then, is to separate truth from lie and decide what to do about it. This is the simple enough in theory, but then, so is sex. To our everlasting benefit, we seem unable to leave simple things be.

DETECTING A LIAR

You've probably told someone that you liked her new haircut when you didn't. It wasn't true but it wasn't really lying. It was one of those convolutions of the truth that make life easier. Research estimates that the average American tells an incredible two hundred lies everyday, including white lies and stock excuses such as, "Sorry I couldn't make it, but I got tied up at the office."

What you need to watch out for are complete falsehoods and the manipulators who fabricate them. The married man who asserts he's free as a bird or the woman who makes up tales of her wealth and status will cause you nothing but frustration and, at times, downright misery. Yet, some people are such convincing artists of deception that it may be hard to see through their facade. Here are some tips that may help you decipher whether or not someone is trying to put one over on you.

Voice inflection. While an inexperienced liar's pitch will elevate, an accomplished liar will lower his tone.

Suspicious eye contact or lack of it. Research indicates that people will glance to the right immediately after telling a falsehood. Someone who won't look you in the eye while talking to you may also be fibbing.

Repetition of a statement. People telling lies frequently repeat them in an attempt to give them credence.

Nervousness. The person with sweaty palms or a flushed face may be rivaling Pinocchio for the all-time lying record.

Also watch out for people who talk too quickly or who frequently pause or falsely stutter.

Restrained gestures. One study showed that people lying tended to use fewer of the casual gesticulations that usually accompany speech—pointing, sketching in the air. Instead, fibbers tend to lick their lips and rub their eyes.

A fixed smile. A liar will try to mask his deceptions with a reassuring grin. But watch out if it disappears too soon or lingers too long.

Abusiveness. A liar may try to proclaim his falsehoods in a loud, forceful manner in an attempt to thwart attempts to challenge him.

IS WHAT THEY SAY, WHAT THEY MEAN?

Ah, consolation. People are so well meaning when they dish out the comforting cliches. But do they mean what they say so well? Let's look at some of the most commonly used feel-better-fast phrases and see what's really behind them:

What They Say

"Don't worry. Everything will be alright."

What They Mean

A) If from a lawyer or doctor, and you trust their opinion—believe it.
B) If from someone with sincerity in their voice, it means, "Don't worry. Everything will be alright."
C) If from someone reading the paper, counting the flies on the ceiling or similarly distracted, it means, "Leave me alone already. I'm tired of hearing your voice." How considerate. How touching.

What They Say

"Don't cry. Nothing is worth getting that upset about."

What They Mean

A) If from someone under the age of 13, accept it as their way of consoling you. They're too young to know better.
B) If from someone over the age of 75, accept it as their way of consoling you. They're too old to remember.

C) If from someone in between in age, either they have the IQ of a gnat, the emotional worries of a log, or they're simply insensitive. You know them, you choose.

What They Say

"Look on the bright side."

What They Mean

A) Perhaps he or she is a scientist calling your attention to a particular phase of the moon. Dead giveaway: if they say this pointing to the sky.
B) Perhaps this is the eternal optimist we've all heard so much about. Do not be concerned. They will learn. Life is obviously just a phase they haven't gone through yet.
C) This is a comedian. Do not take them too seriously. This person makes a living trying to make people laugh. Cut them a break. Laugh.

What They Say

"Things can only get better."

What They Mean

A) A lucky stiff. Go to Vegas, the race track, or a bingo game with them. And bet heavily.
B) A character in a fairy tale. Wake up. You are dreaming. Or watching Saturday morning T.V.
C) A liar. Step on his or her deceitful tongue.

What They Say

"This too shall pass."

What They Mean

A) Words of a prophet. Pay them their fee and go home. Next time you'll know better.
B) Words of a doctor specializing in gallstones or kid-

ney stones. Pay them their fee and go home. Next time
you'll eat better.
C) Words of someone who's obviously never been
through what you're going through. Or else has a lousy
memory. Our advice: take a pass.

What They Say

"Someday, you'll look back at this and laugh."

What They Mean

A) Your chiropractor thinks you can be fixed. The op-
erative word, however, is someday. Good news.
B) Your accountant is trying to tell you you're being
audited. More good news.
C) Your lawyer thinks they'll settle out of court. For
a price. Which you can make in easy monthly payments. Isn't good news fun?

What They Say

"Every cloud has a silver lining."

What They Mean

A) Someone making weather predictions. Take your
umbrella.
B) Someone who's confused reality with optimism.
Take your hip boots.
C) Someone who designs sets for a living. Take your
binoculars.

What They Say

"Time heals all wounds."

What They Mean

A) Maybe their religion doesn't allow them to go to
doctors. Think of what they save on medical bills.
B) Maybe they've only been superficially wounded in
love. Think of what they're saving in Kleenex.

C) Maybe they're the ones time forgot. How else could they have forgotten the pain.?

What They Say

"All's well that ends well."

What They Mean

A) If you're in Texas or Oklahoma, listen carefully to the accent. You may have just struck it rich.
B) If you're in a fairy tale, the story's over. Close the book.
C) When was the last time you had a relationship end well? Obviously this statement is a baldfaced lie.

Of course, there are also some phrases where you know full well what they mean.

"I know what you're going through," means, "I have no idea the depth of pain you're feeling."

"Trust me," means, "Run like hell unless you want to lose your shirt. Or worse."

"Pick you up at 7," generally means, "If I'm there by 8 you're lucky."

"Don't take it so seriously," means, "This is getting too heavy and any second I'll bolt out of your life forever."

"I'll call you," means, "see you around."

"See you around," means, "Around the turn of the century."

And "Take it easy," means, "Have a nice life."

Now that you know what they really mean, you can avoid the traps of believing what they say. Who knows, perhaps with a little practice, you can even become proficient at saying, "Thanks," and "That's okay," when you really mean, "Go to..." well, you get the point.

Flirting

Do you flirt?

If you answered "yes," consider yourself normal. If you answered "no," consider yourself out of touch or comatose.

The fact is, we all flirt almost every day. From the first time you coyly goo-gooed at Mommy or Daddy until that last sly look at the cute salesperson a few hours ago, you have been flirting with your fellow beings and they have been flirting back.

Flirting is a healthy and natural way to enjoy people without taking very big risks. The dictionary (Webster's) defines flirting as "playing at love" and "acting amorously without serious intentions"; just imagine the hot water we would be in if we had to be serious about all those daily teases we enjoy so much! Flirting is an aspect of sexuality that may be a prelude to bigger and better things, but it may also be an end in itself. You might call it playing the game at level two or three instead of level ten. Although we are fortunate to live in an age where coitus does not have to lead to impregnation, the emotional ramifications of the act still remain, and flirting can be a safe outlet for sexual tension.

RULES OF THE GAME

Some people flirt because they enjoy the power they have to make people react. One of their least credible lines is, "I didn't have any idea he/she was taking me seriously!" Ideally, everyone in the flirting game would know what was at stake in each round, but usually one can only try not to mislead or be misled. There are examples of male and female co-workers who flirt in open and casual fashion, using salty language and mannerisms that would seem to indicate that they are making themselves available to each other, even when this is not the case. If a new arrival steps into such a scene, however, he could easily get the wrong impression. If you are going to play hard, be sure you also let it be known that you are only flirting, and not using office time as a prelude to sex.

Although flirting involves just a pinch of our sexual gunpowder, one should be cautious about using it in high-risk situations. You better be sure you have a clear mutual understanding before you flirt with your boss, your best friend's spouse, or your teenage niece or nephew. Test the appropriateness of your urge to flirt by asking yourself the question, "What are my intentions?" Do you really want the flirting to lead to further involvement or not? Beware.

Now let us get on with the business of "serious flirting," that is, flirting that we hope will lead us onward. Here are the basic stages of single-to-single flirtation.

Approach or acknowledgment. Usually called "checking someone out," this is the way you let the other person know you exist and that you are aware they exist. It may be verbal ("Hi") or non-verbal (eye contact, raised eyebrows).

The face-off. In the next step, the people involved position their bodies in a face-to-face position. This gives two potential sexual partners an opportunity to size each other up. It is an open position physically, one in which you may look into the other person's eyes and feel the vibes. Conversation at this stage is generally light and inconclusive; the conclusions being made are non-verbal and will lead to the next step or to the next person.

Synchronization. We tend to imitate the actions of those around us. It is a theatrical axiom that yawning begets yawning and laughter begets laughter; we all know couples whose mannerisms are so similar that we are sure they stay up nights studying each other. A closer look at flirting behavior shows us that couples who are enjoying each other begin at some point to engage in imitative and synchronized behavior. If you are talking together, you may find that you raise your glasses at the same time, you set them down together, you both raise a hand to your face, and so on. This shows physically that you are on the same wave length psychologically. At this stage, what psychologists call "displacement"—the touching of oneself instead of the other person—may take place. So notice when he runs his fingers through his hair or when she tugs at her earlobe!

The first touch. Usually this happens "accidentally." You may lightly touch the person's hand while making a point in conversation, you may brush against her when going for the next round of drinks. If you have not had physical contact prior to that moment, this can be significant— and delicious.

The first touch is sometimes the first stage of flirting, so do not interpret all body contact as a come on. The four-step sequence is a frequently observed pattern but it may change slightly with new partners in new situations. Just remember that serious flirting comes in definite stages. Be alert, stay aware of the stage you are at, and you will be on top of the situation no matter what rules the other person is playing by.

What Is Chemistry?

Chemistry, that compelling and irresistible attraction between strangers that draws them together in an exhilarating frenzy of passion, is perhaps the most wonderful and ethereal phenomenon of romantic love. All of us recall a lover to whom we were instantly and hopelessly attracted. The scene of our first meeting is played again and again in soft focus in our memory.

And chemistry is unexplainable. What clicks between two strangers so suddenly and mysteriously? Is it really love at first sight? Do we predictably respond to the stimulus of the physical type that represents a subliminal image of our perfect Cinderella or Prince Charming?

Any answer that might be offered, say, by modern psychology, medicine or witchcraft, is meaningless because, regardless of the cause, it is here to stay. We must accept the fact of chemistry as a given and move on to theorize about its ultimate effects. We can only hope to understand how certain factors in us work to attract us to others.

Too often, when we go for a "type," we close our eyes to other things. We ignore the deficiencies that make the object of our affections less than right for us. He or she may be less involved in the relationship than we are, but that realization gets lost in the glow.

Interestingly, men are more interested in how a woman *looks* than who she *is*. Although women value external attributes, they place more emphasis on intelligence, power, competence and confidence than do men. After the man and woman have had the opportunity to learn more about each other, it is the man who overlooks his partner's other flaws and remains fascinated by her looks. Women more easily drop men who look good but lack other qualities.

Physical beauty is an inescapable factor in attraction. Regardless of how we may protest that it is a person's inner loveliness that matters, it is the pretty face or the handsome countenance that grabs our attention. Beauty is valued highly in our culture. Studies show that pretty babies are held and cuddled more than their less attractive counterparts. This phenomenon carries over into adult life, witnessed by the proliferation of beauty contests and skin magazines. Some even theorize that the recent trend in physical body fitness is based on a desire to look good rather than feel good.

Just as chemistry is here to stay, our culture's preoccupation with external beauty is equally well-entrenched: we can't change it, but we can see how it figures in the way we view ourselves and others. To admire and desire the beauty of another is, after all, to hold the mirror up to our own attributes.

Physical beauty is connected with our own self-esteem as well as with the image we present to the world. Preoccupation with external qualities lays bare our own insecurities and confusion. The key is that, the more we accept ourselves, the more we learn to accept the less-than-perfect physical characteristics of the pool of potential dates and mates.

The overly critical man or woman who mentally crosses off the unacceptables in the dating pool on the basis of some tiny deficiency may attribute this process to high standards, but the real reason usually lies deeper. What this person is really doing, by setting unreasonably high expectations, is avoiding emotional intimacy by eliminating many possible dates. Or perhaps this person is expressing a fear that others will think less of him or her because of the shortcomings of his or her mate.

Super-attractive people are often viewed by those who fancy them as "unaffordable." The man, for example, who fantasizes about a lovely and untouchable stranger sees himself as having nothing to barter, such as comparable looks, power, money or intelligence to measure up to her beauty. He fears that she will make him feel inferior. This man, by avoiding contact with his dream girl, expresses—but does not deal with—his feelings of inadequacy and fear of being made to feel small by the woman he is with.

Other psychological factors influence our fascination with certain "types." For example, tall men and petite women often couple up to create a sense of dominance/protection. A man may go for a flashy, Hollywood type because she makes him look good when others notice her.

For the same reasons that tall men and short women pair, women of all heights look to tall men as the embodiment of intelligence, authority and competence. A tall man who truly has these qualities is self-assured because he has gotten positive reinforcement from others. Conversely, tall men who do not measure up to the stereotype are fraught with anxieties and self-doubt because others expect too much of them.

Short men, however, must live with the reality that, while they may have many admirable qualities, these attributes are summarily dismissed with the one phrase, "But he's so short." Ironically, it is his Napoleon-like stature that forces the short man to be more aggressive. Short men are often wittier, sexier, more loving and more sensual to compensate for the lack of height that their towering peers posses.

Women who do not view themselves as homecoming queen material, similarly, often develop their minds to overcome their lack of physical beauty. These women may actually be very attractive but suffer from the hopelessly high standard of feminine charm with which they were imprinted as teenagers. When these women pursue careers, the confidence they develop through job success

spills over and they emerge, like the ugly duckling in the fairy tale, into beautiful swans. The combination of beauty, intelligence and self-confidence is threatening to many men who fear that their career-minded mate will outshine, outearn, and outgrow them.

External characteristics aside, it is an innate desire for wholeness that is at the core of our attraction to another. No man is an island, it is said. Each of us has gaps in our character and experience that must be filled in by someone else.

This phenomenon, expressed in the old saw "opposites attract" is better characterized as complementary. It is manifested in the positive tension in a relationship of equal opposites. Partners in this situation can disagree and remain close because they respect the polarity that forms the basis of the attraction in the first instance. They are two different people and not a mirror of each other.

True complementarity is a complex expression of the inter-face between independence and dependence, sensuality and sexual love, active aggression and passivity, and confidence and self-doubt. Often, those who complement each other possess the same vulnerabilities but cope with them in different ways.

For example, neither the one given to high drama and grandstanding nor the partner who remains icily aloof have learned appropriate modes of expressing anger. Both the sexually inhibited and the aggressive lover share the same fear of emotional intimacy.

This polarity can be positive or negative. Obviously, the histrionics of his or her mate will frighten the reserved partner, who will withdraw more and more, intensifying the hysteric's tantrums. The sexually shy partner will label the aggressive one a sex maniac. The "sex fiend" sees his or her timid lover as a cold fish.

There are no-win situations in which the underlying vulnerability makes the relationship impossible. In positive situations, however, the shared vulnerability makes the pairing work. Thus, the miser balances the spendthrift. Both fear that they are not deserving and each handles the conflict in an unsuccessful way. The tightwad loosens up and isn't so hard on himself. The overly generous one tightens the belt and learns inwardly that he is deserving.

These lessons are learned in the context of a healthy, loving relationship that is based on true complementarity. While we may be lucky enough to find that in a person to whom we are drawn by chemistry, it is important to recognize that the balance of two equal opposites is the goal of a good relationship. True and lasting love cannot be based on the external beauty of a partner, but rather on how he or she fills the void in your life.

WHY WELL DRESSED WOMEN TURN MEN ON — OR VICE VERSA

The clothes one wears indicates many things about a person: your economic class, perhaps the kind of work you do, what kind of image you wish to present of yourself. But most important, when your clothes fit well, others will sense that you are proud of your body—and will therefore pay attention to it. If your clothes are stylish and up-to-date, others will know that you are interested in being attractive. Wanting to be attractive and having the confidence to let your desire be known is the better half of sex-appeal. Are you attracted to those who show no concern for their appearance? Probably not. The principles guiding another person's desires are not very different from those which guide your own.

If you're young and in great shape, stylish clothes will only make you even more appealing. If you're older, dressing stylishly will show that you are still young at heart; and your fashionable clothes will reinforce the elegance apppropriate to your station in life.

Be careful what clothes you select. Avoid synthetics; they don't hold their shape as well as natural fibers; they wear out more quickly; and they simply don't look as good. Cotton, wool, and silk are more comfortable than rayon, dacron, or any of their ilk. If you feel unsure of your tastes in fashion, choose whatever suits you best among the items offered by "designer" labels. That way you'll be sure to get modern, fashionable, quality articles.

If you pay attention to the way you dress, your clothes and your bearing will automatically set you apart from others. If you're confident that you are looking your absolute best, others will sense that and be turned on.

III

Travel For Singles

Travel Hot Spots

There are hundreds of locations, each with scores of special spots that will satisfy the holiday desires of singles. Some of them follow, but almost weekly new locations and establishments are being discovered that will become tomorrow's meccas for singles. A travel agent will point you in the right direction. Most holiday places are only five or six hours away from either coast.

The Bahamas: *Nassau.* Nassau is great. The locals are friendly, geared to tourism, and there is an abundance of vacationing singles, most likely some from your own home town. Nassau is loaded with English pubs. You will not be disappointed in any of them, but don't fail to stop at Green Shutters. It's special: helpful, active personnel; a carefee ambiance, and you cannot get to the bar without weaving through dozens of people your own age. Another great locale is the Buena Vista Restaurant. The food is delightful and the charm of the place will leave you with a lasting memory of it.

The Bahamas: Paradise Island. Right across the bridge from Nassau is an extraordinary delight: incredible beach, super sunsets, resplendent sunrises. This is a truly superb setting for singles to meet each other or to contentedly enjoy it with a companion. As for night life, try these:

Flagler Inn: This place is crowded, happy; serves generous drinks, very acceptable food, moderate prices; and is full of bodies, two-thirds of them three-quarters bare.

Loew's: It's not a theater. It's a dynamite cocktail lounge; everything you'll get at Flagler's, but just a bit more sedate. The food's a little better.

The Beach Inn: Ocean, sand, suds and fun characterize this place. During the American happy hour you can get two drinks for the price of one.

Britannia Beach Hotels: You'll find a friendly and very heterogeneous group of people in the cocktail areas here.

Club Med is a great attraction because of its total services. The club here is well known for its orientation toward tennis.

And, if you are attracted to gambling, don't forget that there are some fabulous gambling casinos on the island. Good luck!

Mexico: Acapulco. It has a good reputation and it lives up to it, year after year. Don't worry if you change time zones when you go there. You will more than make it up—if you want to.

There is a lot of afternoon activity here. Venture into Tabasco Beach. It is a beach club next to the *Malibu Hotel*; which is quite a funky place that is very popular with singles. This gathering center rests in the middle of the best bay beach.

Give Condesa Beach a chance to please you. In local circles it is known as the "afternoon beach," a place where people start making plans for the evening. In the immediate area there is also *Pariaso's* and *Beto's*, very good seafood restaurants. There is dancing in front of these establishments and three or four others that are nearby. It is said that general social havoc abounds in this section.

For shopping try *Acapulco Jo*. The *Villa Vera Hotel* is also a very popular place in the hills with a great, fun crowd of people. It's a "happening place." But, don't go there if you are tight on cash; it's expensive. *Carlos 'n Charlie's* has built a reputation for drinking, singing, and meeting people.

Mexico: Puerto Vallarta. Afternoon activity here reaches a high pitch at the south end of the village, along Playa del Sol. Almost everything that is fun goes. On the beach and at the beach bars of major hotels there is dancing, fraternizing, and the wildest, loudest possible music. Here the special places are *Posada Vallarta, Camino Real*, and *Fiesta Americana.* Quite promptly at 6:00 p.m. most singles head for *Carlos O'Brien's, Casablanca,* or *Daiquiri Dick's* for happy hour, called *hora feliz* here. The ambiance, attitude, and setting sun always promise an exceptional evening.

Mexico: Mazatlan: This is the most northerly of Mexican resort cities. It is the closest to the United States; flying time is less. Sabalo Beach is great, almost kinky, and always loaded with friendly people. The terrace of the *Playa Hotel* is the best place to spend an afternoon. For many years this has been a central gathering place: the code word is fun. Economically, *Mazatlan* is the best singles bargain in all Mexico. Cheap, that is, for a big resort city.

Club Med Playa Blanca Village is approximately halfway between Puerto Vallarta and Manzanillo; about a two-hour drive. Not bad; happy hour at *Playa Blanca* lasts well past eight o'clock.

The best seafood in all of Mexico is to be found here. In fact, if you are a sea-loving type, why not charter a deep sea fishing boat of your own? There are plenty of boats, rental gear, and willing skippers to take you a few miles out. If you'd rather eat in a restaurant, the *Playa Mazatlan Hotel* has a great crowd and is very popular. Also, you might try the *Camino Real Hotel* which has a beautiful location and grounds. It's also away from the crowds.

Baja California Peninsula. Manzanillo, Cabo San Lucas, and La Paz, are nice cities, but are not really for singles. These locations are oriented toward families and senior citizens.

Ixtapa. Fly into Zihuatanejo's airport, but stay in Ixtapa, which is a very small town in the suburbs. *Club Med* is here, which helps account for its fast-growing population. There are miles of soft, fine-grained sand lined with palm groves. For shopping drive into Zihuatanejo. You'll find some great bargains.

Guaymas. Another excellent *Club Med* resort is here. One of the key attractions is the fact that Guaymas is so close to California. The desert, mountains, and the beautiful sea make this a beautiful location. However, getting here can be a problem; almost all flights must go through Phoenix.

Hawaii: Maui. During the last several years Maui has become one of the world's most talked-about vacation islands. It seems the perfect place to enjoy the wonderful Hawaiian lifestyle, sun, and beaches. *The Hyatt Maui* is very popular with single people. Their pools alone are worth the visit. *Lahaina Village* is a wonderful place to walk and shop. There is a fun bar crowd and loads of great restaurants. Something to think about when making your room reservations is the possibility of getting yourself a condo. If you want to share a place with several friends, this can be a great bargain. If you want to spend your time with someone very special, condo living on Maui can make it that much more romantic.

and you may hear many renditions of the score from "South Pacific." Local musicians are everywhere, they seem to pop out from behind trees. They're good. And friendly. They'll even welcome you to sing along or try their guitar.

In Tahiti, you are suddenly cast in the middle of nature's purity. A first impression is that your eyesight has improved. You can see so far. There's no haze. Objects miles away become clearly outlined. Tahiti is clean, pure, smogless, pretty much as it was at the beginning. And in a glass-bottom boat or swimming you can see twenty feet down. If you are curious about fish, you will be able to see dozens fear below your toes.

Tahiti draws a very heterogeneous contingency of tourists. It is not specifically set up for singles, but they abound, are laid-back, easy to meet, and ready for festive fun.

Tahiti: Bora Bora. Very primitive. Down to the essentials, like nudity on some of the beaches—in the daytime. There are many Hollywood people here—the real thing. Bora Bora is a much-favored location for many film-production companies. Something is always shooting, it seems. And at night, you'll mingle with cast and crew, dance, sing, eat and drink well, make friends quickly, skinny dip, and become part of a wondrous night.

Dirt roads abound here. There are lots of bikes and wilderness trails. And, the snorkling is fantastic!

Tahiti: Morea. This island heaven is almost a twin of Bora Bora, but one item makes it stand out: *Harry's Bar.* (No relation to the one in Venice.)

This is the meeting place for singles; in fact, it is almost exclusively singles. There are no formalities. You go there to meet people, raise hell. And that you'll do. It opens early, around 7:00 a.m., if the employees make it after partying all night. If they don't, you can get in around nine or ten. Bikini swimsuits for the ladies and bikini briefs for the men are appropriate attire. The posture is semi-prone, the attitude extremely casual, just as long as it keeps you having one heck of a good time. Darts is the most energetic formal sport at Harry's. The bets are sometimes high, and have nothing at all to do with money.

Check out the *Hotel Kia Ora* and its "floating bar." A few years ago somebody commandeered an old wooden ship and anchored it in the harbor.

COLD CLIMATE HOT SPOTS

Aspen, Colorado. Little can be added to the legend of Aspen. It embraces every cold weather adjective, is a love affair with dreams, and seduces women and men who are single.

Skiing, of course, is the thing. But so is shopping. If singles aren't on the slopes, sitting around a fireplace, or meeting at the bars and lounges, they are shopping.

Boutiques and shops compete for space on the narrow streets of Aspen. They're everywhere. And as you window shop, buy, or bump into other singles, there is a paradoxical sensation that comes over you. This is a jet-set center. People—even royalty—come to Aspen from every part of the world. But Aspen is also quaint and has the feel of a home town; it is probably this that makes it such an exceptional holiday spot for singles.

Be prudent in the shops; the same item is about fifty percent higher here than in a department store at home.

Deer Valley, Utah. Fly into Salt Lake City and drive the thirty-five minutes to Deer Valley. This area is now being referred to as the "Aspen of Utah." There are great slopes for all levels. The fantastic *Stein Erikson Lodge* is something to write home about.

But it's all together at Aspen, a winter-resort that singles must attend at least once while still single.

Ketchum, Idaho. This place has only very recently been discovered by unmarried men and women. It is famous as the home of Ernest Hemingway. (He divided time somewhat equally between Havana and Ketchum, during

Castro days. It is here that he prowled the streets at night, his paranoia growing—lights in a bank, to him, meant the IRS was scrutinizing his tax report—and it was in Ketchum that he committed suicide with a twelve-gauge shotgun.)

In Ketchum, don't fail to have a drink at *Marty's*. The place is new but the setting is historic. This is the gathering place for singles who have come to Ketchum for hunting—pheasants mostly—fishing, or a look at Middle America.

Mammoth. Some fantastic skiing happens here. It's crowded and that will either be a plus (if you want to meet people), or a minus (if you want to ski a lot). *The Whiskey-Creek Bar and Restaurant* is a "must visit."

CRUISES

Windjammer Cruises. Travel to many islands in the Caribbean on a tall wooden ship. A private company, Windjammer, has seven different ships that try to provide both laid-back luxury and a more intimate style of traveling; quite different from the large ocean cruisers.

S.S. Azure Seas. Mostly for the Southern California crowd, these three- or four-night cruises are really "party boats." Perhaps the best way to explain the uniqueness of these cruises is that with only three or four days to enjoy the ocean, people really try to pack in as much fun as possible.

Senior-World Cruises. Operated by Gramercy Travel of New York, these are for the over-45 set, married or single. Even if you are going alone and don't want to pay the stiff single-supplement, they will arrange for shared accomodations to keep the cost down.

Commodore Cruise Line. Their ship, "Caeibe," reserves approximately twenty-five percent of their cabins

for singles. And, the cost is one-half the cost of double occupancy.

Gramercy's Singleworld. This is the largest company
dealing exclusively in the singles market. (444 Madison
Avenue, New York, NY 10022)

Companions in Travel. This organization will match
you with a roommate at no cost. (1194 Oakfield Avenue,
Wantagh, NY 11793)

Solo Flights. They act for singles, both as a travel center and as a travel and social club. (8 Washington Avenue,
Westport, CT 06880)

Tips On Traveling

Traveling alone, whether for business or pleasure,
can be an adventure or a real drag. What can make it
more the first and less the latter?

Getting down to business, men have traditionally been
the experts in the arena of business traveling. But with
more women in the workforce, there are also more wom-
en on the road, and the hotels are gradually adjusting to
suit them. For instance, women travelers will find more
and more special accomodations—floors designated for
women only, suites that separate the bedroom from the
living room, making business meetings in the hotel room
more comfortable. Hotels have even increased security,
using computerized keys and surveillance cameras.

Service in other areas has improved, too. Waiters now are paying more attention to the business woman. They no longer assume the man in the party automatically gets the wine list, or the check. The more women travel on business, the more the hotels will be inspired to cater to women, too.

And just because you're traveling alone, it doesn't mean you have to stay alone on the road. You can make new business connections, not to mention romantic connections, if you have the right attitude. People do tend to have a different attitude when they travel. Whether it's the anonymity of being in a new city, the comraderie of the road, or the short duration of the trip, traveling seems to make people more open to adventure. And that includes adventures of the heart.

To meet people on the road, you may have to change some of your habits and let yourself do things you wouldn't ordinarily do at home. The most important thing to remember is not to stay in your room. Eat in the hotel dining room, out in a restaurant nearby, or one you've heard about from other travelers. Ask the waiter to put you at a table near other single people. Start up a conversation. They'll probably welcome it, in fact. Few people really like to eat alone.

After dinner, if you have nothing to do, don't do nothing. Go to the hotel bar. Even if you'd never set foot in a bar alone at home, remember, you're not at home now. Befriend the bartender, and he or she will most likely help steer trouble away. That should make you feel more comfortable about talking to strangers. And just because you talk to someone, don't feel pressured to leave with them unless you want to. Keep in mind that not everyone you'll talk to is after romance. Maybe they're just looking for an evening's conversation and a little companionship.

Assuming you don't have friends in the town you're traveling to, you can also stay busy by making plans with the people you're doing business with. Ask them to dinner or drinks at the end of the day and maybe you won't have to head for the hotel alone.

Once you've met people, it never hurts to stay in touch.

If they travel as much as you do, you may end up in the same city again soon, and you'll have someone to see the town with. Of course, you could always make plans to meet on purpose, giving you yet another reason to pack your bags.

Which brings us to another type of travel—the fun type—vacation. Have you ever skipped a vacation because you didn't have anyone to go with? You're not alone. But it's not a healthy practice. Everyone needs time off and, more importantly, time away, a real break from the grind. No matter how much you like your work, you always do better when you've gotten a respite and a rest. Traveling alone is neither unheard of nor as scary as you might think. For the newly initiated and extremely intimidated, there are always the prepackaged plans, like cruises or Club Med.

But for those who want to have a true adventure, exploring the country, even foreign countries can be fascinating. Don't worry about the language. Get a Berlitz record from the library and practice a little before you leave. Arm yourself with a pocket dictionary. Lose your inhibitions about pointing and gesturing. Most natives are eager to help you make yourself understood once you've displayed an interest in their homeland. You may even find yourself taken under someone's wing, and gaining the best kind of tour guide there is.

Get a good map and go exploring on your own. Need help finding your way around? Ask your hotel clerk for directions. That's what they're there for.

Feel like you're playing Monopoly with foreign money? Buy a pocket converter that will tell you how to convert amounts in local currency into dollars. Watch the financial section before you leave so you learn how the currency at your destination is fluctuating. Call your bank for information. Speaking of banks: they tend to give you the best rate of exchange for your money. Your hotel doesn't.

For safety's sake, keep your domestic and foreign currency separate. You won't get them confused that way. And keep a record of the serial numbers on your traveler's checks separate from the checks. In the event of theft, you'll have the number to report so you can get your money back.

Also, leave your room key at the front desk when you leave the hotel. It's easy enough to pick it up when you come back and you won't need it until then anyway. This safeguards against loss.

Getting sick at home is no fun. It's even less fun abroad. But there are some helpful hints to minimize the suffering. Bring a small medical kit with you—the kind that has a thermometer, band aids, aspirin, diarrhea remedy, and stomachache reliever in it. Sunscreen, sunburn ointment, bug repellent, and calamine lotion could be useful if you're planning a vacation to a hot spot.

If you get sick beyond what your emergency kit can handle, your hotel manager can always find you a doctor who speaks English. And it's generally not impossible to find American over-the-counter drugs overseas, either in a city pharmacy or one attached to an American hotel chain. If you are taking prescription medication when you leave the states, be sure to bring enough to last (even outlast) your stay. And bring your doctor's prescription as a just-in-case, or to prove at customs that you're supposed to have the drugs.

Above all, keep in mind that you're not going to another planet, just another country. You may actually find yourself enjoying traveling alone. After all, you've got your freedom, you go where you want to, when you want to, and see the sights you want to. If you want to move on to another city sooner than planned, you can. If you want to stay longer, it's your choice. You never know who you can meet. And if you do meet someone, being on your own lets you call the shots. Which can turn a vacation into the time of your life.

Safety Reminders

When you are planning a vacation, safety—your own and that of your belongings—is the last thing you want to worry about. But do not wait until the last minute to start thinking about protecting yourself and your apartment or house. Start planning in advance.

Before you leave. Tips on how to leave your apartment or house when departing on a vacation are well publicized, and frequently overlooked. They are worth repeating.

1. Alert some neighbors. Let them know how long you will be gone. If they see activity around your place, hear the stereo blasting, or observe anything out of the ordinary, they will call the police.

2. Hook some lights up to a timer, or arrange for someone to turn some out and others on every night.

3. Temporarily stop newspaper delivery. Make sure someone will get rid of the throwaway newspapers and ads that will collect in front of your house or at the door of your apartment.

4. If you live in a house, call the local police and tell them how long you will be away. If you have an apartment, let management and the security force know.

5. If appropriate, do leave things around your place to make it look lived in while it's not.

6. Check the fire alarms in your home before departing. Make sure they work. Even the best batteries

wear out and there can be malfunctions. Although you will not be there to hear the alarm if it goes off, a near neighbor might.

Traveling safely. There is an abundance of information and specialized products to protect you while traveling and during your vacation. Following are ten especially good hints.

1. Safety pouches and money belts are good ideas. They wrap around your waist under your clothing. Some weigh only three ounces. Enclose traveler's checks, money, passport, and other valuables inside the pouch. (The item can be ordered for $6.95 from Eddie Bauer, Department AM9, Fifth and Union, Seattle, WA 98124 (216) 622-2766.)

2. Travel light. If a single carry-on bag will do it for you, your potential luggage loss is greatly reduced. And you will have less to worry about, will feel freer, and will have more fun.

3. Crowded places, such as airports, are the working environment for pickpockets and luggage thieves. Do not become distracted; keep a watch on your luggage. Women can clutch their purses tightly without announcing exactly where their money is; men should be sure they only mentally clutch their wallets. Men touch their wallets when they see a sign that says "beware of pickpockets." Pickpockets are good observers, and will learn from this which pocket a man's wallet is in.

4. Thieves can be discouraged if you hang a lightweight cordless electric door alarm on the inside doorknob of your hotel room door. If there is hanky-panky by a thief and someone tries to enter, a piercing, high-decibel alarm sounds. (Can be purchased for $24.95. Order from Hammacher Schlemmer by phone, (800) 228-5656. Ask for style number N-154.)

5. As soon as you check into a hotel or other vacation quarters, locate and memorize the nearest fire exit

and an alternate. It will only take a minute or two and can save your life.

6. Smoke alarms are required at most places, but do not depend on them entirely. Sometimes they don't work. For about thirty dollars at most houseware stores, a portable smoke alarm can be purchased. Simply hang it on the inside doorknob of your room, plug it in, and sleep safely confident that you are protected during the night.

7. Never talk loudly about your travel plans in detail in public. Criminals like to hear such information. It gives them an edge over you.

8. When using credit cards, be certain they are returned to you. And be sure it is your own that's returned. Personnel in shops and restaurants are often rushed and will not notice such a mistake right away.

9. Practically every city and town in the world has both safe and unsafe areas. Stay away from the latter. Ask at your hotel's desk, or check with police.

10. The center or near-center of a sidewalk is the best place to walk. If you are near the street, a thief in a vehicle can snatch your purse. If you are on the inside, someone could grab your handbag from a building doorway or an alley.

IV

Relationships

Is Falling In Love
Another Media Hype?

Birds do it, bees do it, or do they? We've all grown up believing in love. Given it mystical powers. The power to cure. To conquer all. To make the world go round. But love does not exist everywhere in the world.

A story is told of some anthropologists who went to an island and described to the natives what it was like to be passionately in love, all the stuff from the movies—your hearts beat fast, you have sweaty palms, and you can't concentrate because you keep thinking about that other person; everything we associate with infatuation—and do you know what the natives did? They just laughed. Their one comment was something to the effect of, "You're describing someone who's crazy."

Indeed, that comparison has been made a lot. How often have you heard someone say, "I'm just crazy about him-/her/you"? And yet, no one carts that person off to a room where they can safely bounce off the four walls until that feeling has passed. Instead, that feeling is encouraged. By love songs, movies, ads (you can even be crazy about a product, ask any advertiser).

But is the heart-pounding, toe-tingling, not-eating, sleeping-or-thinking feeling truly love, or is it just infatuation, an early unevolved version?

How can you tell the difference? The dictionary says that infatuation is, "to be made foolish or fatuous, to be deprived of sound judgment." So it follows, if you feel like a fool, it must be infatuation. There are those who would say infatuation is when you love the idea of the person, and real love is when you love the person himself or herself. This entails admiration, respect, and an emotional intensity in addition to "the hots" of infatuation.

So what's wrong with infatuation? Nothing, as long as you don't confuse it with love and expect it to last. Infatuation can be fun, and after all, love hasn't always existed as we know it today. A woman in Athens during the classical age would more often than not be married off to an experienced, sometimes reluctant suitor, generally twice her age. Beyond being indifferent to her, very often he held the wedding ceremony without her.

Rome, on the other hand, wasn't much better. Men there lusted after slaves and whores. Wives were affectionately placed on pedestals. Other men's wives, however, were fair game, almost objects of a sport, as Ovid wrote.

In fact, romantic love wasn't even in existence until the twelfth century when a group of medieval crusaders influenced by the Arab culture they had encountered decided to revolt against the church. Then along came King Arthur, Lancelot, Guinevere and their elaborate tales of passion, heroism, and adventure, and *voila*! romantic love. It thrived, not surprisingly, during the romantic age of the nineteenth century, due in part to the violent revolution in France, Napoleon and Josephine (two role models for romance if role models ever existed), and the invention of perfume.

Romanticism actually found its first expression in writers proclaiming their anti-revolutionary devotion. Chateaubriand while exiled, Victor Hugo, and the English poets Byron, Keats, and Shelley led a whole generation in new ways of perceiving relationships.

They raised some important questions about the nature of love, questions people are still trying to answer today.

"Is love blind? Or just wearing glasses?" Think about it for a minute. Isn't being in love really like putting a magnifying glass on the object of your affection? Never are you so fascinated with someone, so obsessed with knowing everything there is to know about them as you are when you're in love. Mere friends do not rate this kind of attention. You see every virtue, every beauty, every delight blown up a thousandfold. You also see every flaw in complete detail, too, but because you are completely taken with that person, the good far outweighs the bad.

Is being in love a drive to make this relationship the center of your life? In a word, yes. Or in the words of Pierre Teilhard de Chardin, "Love alone is capable of uniting living beings in such a way as to complete and fulfill them, for it alone takes them and joins them by what is deepest in themselves." Why then does this feeling of being in love fade? One explanation is that you can't keep up all that kind of intensity forever. Others assert that love is capable of renewal every time your loved one does something admirable. It's enhanced by years of meeting life's challenges, making it through fate's pitfalls, and years of being together. Recharged by each individual's passion for life itself. Choose the view you prefer. But don't be like La Rochefoucauld, the French moralist and not one of history's great romantics, who believed that men would never have loved had they never heard of love. Choose love. Sing a song. Buy a greeting card.

Saying It With Flowers

Flowers! Beautiful, fragrant, personal, they are a perfect gift. But, must you always send the same red rose? Historically, certain flowers mean different things; a short glossary of the "hidden language of flowers" is below. If you give a flower upside down you reverse the meaning.

Forget-me-not, yellow-blue	*true love*
Fuchsia, scarlet	*fast*
Gardenia, white	*secret untold love*
Honeysuckle, yellow	*bonds of love*
Ivy, green	*friendship, fidelity, marriage*
Jasmine, white	*amiability, transports of joy, sensuality*
Leaves, autumn, all colors	*melancholy*
Lilac, purple	*first emotions of love*
Lilac, white	*youthful innocence*
Lilac, white	*purity, sweetness*
Lily of the valley, white	*return of happiness*
Magnolia, waxy white	*dignity, perserverance*
Marigold, yellow	*jealous*
Mint, green	*virtue*
Orange blossom, lightly orange	*your purity equals your loveliness*
Orchid, all colors	*beauty, magnificence*
Pansy, all colors	*thoughts*

Peach blossom, bright pink	*I am your captive*
Petunia, all colors	*your presence soothes me*
Poppy, white	*sleep*
Rose, any color	*love*
Rose, deep red	*bashful shame*
Rose, single, pink	*simplicity*
Rose, thornless, any color	*earthy attachment*
Rose, white	*I am worthy of you*
Rose, withered,white	*transient impressions*
Rose, yellow	*decrease of love,jealousy*
Rosebud, white	*girlhood, am a heart ignorant of love*
Rosemary, gray-green leaves, blue flower	*remembrance*
Sunflower, yellow	*haughtiness*
Tulip, red	*declaration of love*
Tulip, yellow	*hopeless love*
Violet, blue	*faithfulness*
Violet, white	*modesty*
Violet, yellow	*rural happiness*
Zinnia, all colors	*thoughts of absent friends*

Women say it with flowers. There's no threat to a man's masculinity when he receives a bouquet of gorgeous flowers; he loves it. And the woman who send their man (or men) flowers shows her sensual and sensitive side. Flowers can be a real turn on to a man, especially the day after a first date; it's a terrific way to say, "Thank you, I had a great time with you!"

Deciding where to send your gift is important. Should you send them to him at work, the impact of the arrival and display will cause him adulation from fellow employees, or it might embarrass him, so think it over.

Most men say that getting flowers at work makes their day, and because you have made them feel good their productivity usually goes way up (provided that they can keep their mind off you!)

How To Write A Love Letter

W.C. Fields might have been hard-hearted enough to hate kids and kick dogs, but even he was probably reduced to putty by the sublime power of the written word of love. With a love letter, a few scratches of the pen can transform a plain piece of paper into a magic carpet, whisking two lovers far away from everyday cares, out into the ineffable ethers of distant stars; from the burdensome weight of measured reality to the exhilaration of timeless infinity; from lunch at Ketchie's Stand to dinner at the Bistro to Breakfast at Tiffany's; From Here To Eternity.

Truly, this is the stuff which dreams (and movies) are made of. With a love letter, we behold an unmatched potential for romance and fantasy at its purest, an opportunity to link our love with the strength, the majesty and the mystery of the universe.

Unfortunately, we also behold a generation of men and women who are, in large part, afraid to put pen in hand unless they are making a shopping list, doing a crossword, writing a memo or taking dictation. Writing skills seems to have disappeared as a part of high school and college curriculum sometime during the sixties, and those exquisitely wrought 10-page outpourings of love's passion redefined have turned into 3-minute conference calls. Happily though, even the school system's laxity and Ma Bell's distaste for perfumed stationery do not affect our quest for love, and so long as there is love, there will be love letters, even if fewer in number and with more grammatical mistakes. And it is this Almanac's solemn advice that you partake of this most heady of love's nectars.

Yes, even you can write a love letter to make his/her head spin, heart flutter, skin tingle and clothes come off. You may even surprise yourself and rediscover the poet you thought you left behind in knee pants. After all, love (and yes, even lust) is that time of life when we burst the emotional shackles and constraints of everyday civilization and follow the mad rush of our feelings, wherever that may lead. Many of us even live through this, and if you want to do it properly and have something to tell your grandchildren, a love letter is definitely in order. Else, it's like leaving the cherry off the sundae.

But, if you begin to grow cold in the toes when you contemplate the actual sitting-down-and-doing of this dread task—relax! This handy guide shall lead you by the hand through any and every difficulty, showing you how to pick the roses without fear of the thorns, and shall even kick you in the seat if you start to chicken out before it's finished.

WHEN TO WRITE A LOVE LETTER

Any time. Now is a good time, in fact. Yesterday would have been even better, and astrological conjunctions indicate tomorrow will be just dandy.

Actually, there are two ideal times for that special someone to receive a "billet doux": (1) when s/he expects it, and (2) when s/he doesn't expect it. Just as love knows no special season, so does its expression in a letter. There are loving couples who leave each other tender and naughty notes three or four times a day for years. This keeps a spark alive in their relationship. You can send a clever letter to someone you don't know but would like to, a telegram to that intriguing new person in the office next door, a note stuffed inside his/her Sunday paper after an especially nice first date, an impassioned ode to make up after a quarrel, or you can scrawl those three little words on a Kleenex for when s/he needs to blow the nose. A love note need not be a dramatic, traumatic or out-of-the-ordinary undertaking; think of it as a simple way of saying, "You and Me, Kid." And, even in the unthinkable event that your affection is not returned in kind, your manner of expression will be endearing because of its thoughtfulness and because, after all, everybody likes to receive love letters. So take the plunge at every opportunity; the water is always invigorating.

WHAT TO WRITE

Love letters come in all shapes and sizes—short, long, funny, serious, clever, hopelessly romantic, shockingly sexual and pure as winter's snow. What the best ones have in common is the feeling that the author is impassioned beyond mortal bounds, that he/she cannot help but write that letter, that God above has moved his/her hand. The effect upon the reader should be to make him/her feel wonderfully special, separate from the rest of the pack, as if he/she is the only thought in your entire world. Here are some suggestions for different kinds of letters.

The Poetic Letter. True love makes poets of us all, and a true poet can make anyone feel like a lover. If that special someone makes you want to dance and sing, don't resist—head for your writing desk immediately and let your passions flow onto the page.

In this type of letter, it is often effective to choose images that isolate you and your lover along with the grandeur of nature or the mystery of eternity. The resulting metaphor will imply a specially romantic connection between your love and life itself, as for example, "the moon, the stars and us." Corny as it may appear to the rational eye, this sort of imagery, in one form or another, has filled poems and songs from the beginning of time.

Another technique is to expose the utter power of love's hold on you, as Napoleon did in his letter to Josephine. You need not fear putting such potentially dangerous sentiments down on paper; they are not legally binding. Henry VIII once wrote something of this nature to Anne Boleyn and managed to have her beheaded a few year later, anyway. Here is a good example:

"The more I have known you the more have I lov'd. In every way—even my jealousies have been agonies of Love, in the hottest fit I ever had I would have died for you."

John Keats to Fanny Scott

Finally, use the passion of the moment to create new images, fresh and daring means of expression that no lover before you e'er had courage or imagination to explore. Remember, love knows no bounds.

Quickies. You may be one of those strong, silent types who feels uncomfortable and out of character gushing out long declarations of love. Good. Write short ones. How about:

"You/Me." This was used very effectively by an acquaintance of mine after a first date.

"Love you, miss you, must have you, see you tonight." You might even send this as a telegram to his/her office. This unexpected arrival, with its terse, direct approach can be devastating.

A romantic photograph of two lovers in an unbelievably beautiful setting, with the only words being, "Us-Forever."

With love letters, you can often maximize the excitement by minimizing the verbiage. Remember that it is the image you create that counts, and a picture may be worth a thousand words—or the right word can paint a thousand pictures. Make your brevity the soul of wit.

Be Creative. Do not feel that your written declaration of everlasting and unbounded passion must be confined by any kind of writing instrument, any pre-existing language form or any commonly recognized day of the year. We all know that love is not of this earth, so you may just as easily write with lingonberry nectar and a janitor's mop on the side of your friend's pet alligator and date it September 32nd. True, you may write it longhand or type it and simply send it through the mail, but it is often the extra touch of daring, creativity or downright lunacy that will set your effort apart from the rest. There is one case of a painted shoe being sent through the mail, the beloved one's proper address neatly printed on the heel and a delicious love letter laced inside the tongue! And it is always an endearment to write a brief "I love you" or something similar on your arm and then roll up your sleeve when s/he greets you. This kind of bodily inscription is one of the original ideas behind the art form known as tattoo.

If you do choose the more traditional stationery approach, try writing with a special pen, stylized letters or, if you have an artistic bent, a combination of words and drawings. Any extra efforts you put into it will be appreciated. You may send it special delivery, accompanied by flowers, candy, a puppy or any other kind of gift. You may slip it under the door along with a key to your apartment, you may set it to music and place it on the piano, stuff it inside a fortune cookie, inscribe it on the head of a pin, paint it on the dining room ceiling, a twenty-foot billboard or over the blue expanse of the morning sky with a fleet of skywriters.

But write! And you will join those who have discovered that only love's words unchained can connect your feelings to that which no words can express.

Famous Before-and-After Quotes

Diana Dors, about her first husband, Dennis Hamilton:
  Before. If I am subdued, he woos me gently. If I am gay, his lovemaking is boisterous and wild. When he takes me in his arms, I forget everything and give myself to him joyfully and unstintingly.
  After. Let's face it. He was over-sexed!

Lucile Ball, about Desi Arnaz, her husband of nineteen years:
  Before. I fell in love with him on sight. He is the boss, and I like it that way.
  After. The children's school ratings went down. I was told they were showing symptoms of troubled home life. So I told my little daughter about our split-up and they stopped having nightmares.

Marilyn Monroe, about her second husband, Joe di Maggio:
  Before. A man's career is wonderful and exciting.
  After. All he did was watch cowboys on television.

Rita Hayworth, about husband number one, Edward Judson:
> *Before.* I eloped with him because he is everything a girl dreams about. No other man could have made me dye my hair red and reduce by thirty pounds.
> *After.* He treated me as if I had no mind or soul of my own.

About husband number two, Orson Welles:
> *Before.* This is strictly the good thing.
> *After.* I just couldn't take his genius any more.

About husband number three, Aly Khan:
> *Before.* My prince of princes.
> *After.* Aly Khan can do as he pleases. I'm through.

About husband number four, Dick Haymes:
> *Before.* I will follow him anywhere in the world.
> *After.* I don't know where he is and I don't care.

Margaret Leighton, about Laurence Harvey:
> *Before.* It's a crazy sort of relationship, but somehow we will make it work, I am only seven years older than he is.
> *After.* I think it would have broken up even if we hadn't been in show business. And, of course, there is a seven-year difference in our ages.

Duke of Newcastle about wife number one, Jean Banks:
> *Before.* I am very smitten. I fell in love with her as soon as I saw her.
> *After.* Her ideas about associating with other men were far different from mine.

About his second marriage
> *Before.* My family motto is "Loyalty Knows No Shame."
> *After.* He agreed that he had committed adultery at the Dorchester Hotel, London, with the wife of a Cypriot harbormaster.

Zsa Zsa Gabor about husband number one, Turhan Bey:
   Before. I said, "You promised me you'd marry me when I was grown-up. Look! I'm 15." He married me.
   After. I wasn't grown-up, that's for sure. I was bored.

About Mustafa Kermal Ataturk, founder of Modern Turkey:
   Before. He was a prince of lovers—half human, half god.
   After. He was an old man. I have no regrets. I amused him in his last months.

About husband number two, Conrad Hilton:
   Before. Such a lovely lump of a diamond ring. He's a sugar lump.
   After. I never hate a man enough to give him back his diamonds.

About husband number three, George Sanders:
   Before. I am so in love with him.
   After. The trouble was, we were both in love with him.

Ingrid Bergman, about husband number one, Dr. Peter Lindstrom:
   Before. We were just too happily married. What more could a woman ask for?
   After. Poor Peter stands alone in the ruins of our marriage. I just can't help loving Roberto.

About husband number two, Roberto Rosselini:
   Before. I scream at him in Swedish. He screams at me in Italian. We love each other madly. He is alive and makes me alive.
   After. I feel sorry for the men I marry. Roberto and I were really too different.

Brigitte Bardot, about husband number one, Roger Vadim:
   Before. He guides me, sustains me and teaches me to be courageous.
   After. I like my husband, but I like Jean-Louis better.

About Jean-Louis Trintignant:
> *Before.* I will marry him as soon as he is free.
> *After.* He has been called up. I need a man at my side to console me.

About Sacha Distel:
> *Before.* I love him because he is tender with me. His music enthralls me. I am very happy.
> *After.* I have severed all connections with Distel.

About husband number two, Jacques Charrier:
> *Before.* I love him so much. His pain is my pain. (He had appendicitis at the time.)
> *After.* He was such a problem.

Elizabeth Taylor, about husband number one, Conrad Nicholson Hilton, Jr.:
> *Before.* He understands me as a woman. He understands me as an actress.
> *After.* After I married him I fell off my pink cloud with a thud. I have lost weight and can only eat baby food.

About husband number two Michael Wilding:
> *Before.* I feel wonderful. I proposed to him because he had everything I admire in a man. I just want to be with Michael—to be his wife.
> *After.* I'm going to get a divorce. I have an Irish temper and when I explode I explode. I will retire from pictures when I marry Mike Todd.

About husband number three, Mike Todd, later killed in an air crash:
> *Before.* There'll be nobody else.
> *After.* I am so happy that Eddie (Fisher) has got his divorce. I nearly passed out with joy when I heard the news.

Richard Burton, about his second wife, Elizabeth Taylor (her fourth and sixth)
> *Before.* Elizabeth's body is a miracle of construction and the work of an engineer of genius.
> *After.* She is too fat and her legs are too short.

How To Date Many People At The Same Time

Dating a variety of people can be a fun, fulfilling adventure. Many men and women revel in the excitement and personal growth of developing loving friendships with others whose lifestyles and interests differ from their own.

Multiple dating has its pitfalls, though. There is the obvious risk of overlap of time and space set aside for individual lovers. And there is the very real danger of emotional burnout. But these and other obstacles can be averted by the man or woman who is willing to live by a few basic rules.

Number one rule is "be honest." First, be honest with yourself. Are you, by dating a multitude of others, setting a habit pattern that will be impossible to break when you are ready to establish a monogamous relationship? This is really the number one pitfall, as well as the number one rule, of playing the field.

Second, be honest with your lovers. Explain your position at the outset of a dating relationship so that each new friend knows that he or she may not be the only lover in your life. By making this clear from the beginning, you minimize the possibility of tears and trauma when your "infidelity" is discovered later on.

And when your lovers know that the relationship with you is not exclusive, they will be less likely to call or drop by unexpectedly or ask questions that you do not want to answer. Basically, honesty with your lover at the beginning avoids dishonesty later. If your dates all know that

119

their relationship with you may not be exclusive, you are less likely to find yourself enmeshed in a web of subterfuge.

Once you have stated your preference for multiple dating, drop the subject. Never flaunt your other relationship to your lady or gentlemen of the moment. It is unfair and unwise to make your lovers compete.

Some men and women who practice multiple dating avoid embarassing encounters by frequenting different places and engaging in different activities with each lover. A telephone answering machine or an answering service can also take messages from one love as you woo another.

Be prepared that, despite your initial honesty, a lover may give you an ultimatum and insist on an exclusive relationship. If your feelings for this person are intense, rethink your priorities and decide if you're ready for a monogamous relationship. If you are, commit to it and sever your other ties with an honest, face-to-face explanation of the reason for the break-up.

If, after some soul searching, you conclude that you are unwilling to forsake all others, explain this to your friend. Emphasize that you would like to continue seeing him or her but that the relationship will not be your only one. Do not try to humor him or her, saying that your affair will be exclusive when in fact it will not. Don't try to spare your friend's feelings by saying that you may commit to him or her in the future: your lover will misinterpret your meaning. Be unequivocal.

Don't let your social life become an occupation. Balance your lovers around your own lifestyle and time schedule.   Do not allow any of your lovers to put unreasonable demands on you.

For many, the excitement and challenge of maintaining a variety of lovers can be a positive adventure. Meeting and interacting with many types of people promotes personal growth through exposure to new ideas and experiences, which will make you a more interesting mate when you are ready for an exclusive relationship.

Long-Distance Dating

Women your love lives nearby, you both enjoy convenience, community ties, and greater intimacy through frequent contact. But, although having your lover close by is nice, it is not always possible. In today's mobile society, singles from cities and towns hundreds of miles apart meet, date, and fall in love. The message is, if you can sustain the relationship do not let geographic inconvenience inhibit you.

There are some advantages to a long-distance love affair. Because your time together is limited, you focus on each other when you are together and make the relationship number one priority. You are unlikely to plan separate activities, activities with others, or put the relationship on "hold" while your lover is in town.

You will both be on your best behavior to make the most out of time together. A trip to your lover's city can be a mini-vacation with fun and relaxation together as the object. But you should be careful you don't form an unrealistic image of your lover. If your impression is based on limited experience, your lover could be really very different from the way you perceive him or her.

Sex is more intense when it is infrequent. Although it may take longer to get to know each other sexually, sex is less likely to become routine. To bridge the gap, talk about your sexual needs and desires over the telephone. Your lover will eagerly anticipate seeing you again to experiment with all the ways to tease and delight you that you have revealed.

Your relationship will develop at a slower pace, thus buffering the intensity and the risk of burn-out that characterize new relationships. Because you simply will not see each other, or even talk with each other as often, you will be forced to put the reins on those emotional needs that you rely on your lover to fulfill.

There are plenty of disadvantages, too. Long distance love affairs can die from lack of nourishment and shared experiences. A faraway lover is not as integrated into your daily life as he or she would be if the two of you lived close to each other.

Your lover may be married. Beware of a man or woman who will see you only in your city, will not give you a home telephone number, and can rarely spend holidays or weekends with you. If you do not object to dating a married person, go ahead, but make sure your lover is honest about his or her marital status.

The long distance romance can be an unhealthy vehicle to circumvent emotional intimacy. The man or woman who lives far away from his or her lover can easily avoid dealing with the more difficult aspects of a relationship. And face it, if your lover lives far, far away, he or she cannot be there for you when you need someone.

Long distance *can* work. Where both parties are equally committed to sustaining the relationship, the geographic barriers can be conquered.

Ask yourself, "Is this person special enough for me to accept the disadvantages of a long distance affair?" If the answer is yes, expect whopping telephone bills, but enjoy!

When You Feel Ambivalent About A Relationship

So this is it. You're in love. You gaze into each other's eyes for hours, saying more by eye contact than you could in a thousand words. You hug and kiss and hold hands and snuggle and cuddle for hours. At last! This is just what you've wanted, waited for, struggled for so many years. But wait a minute! There's a bit of ambiguity here. Pretty soon you look at your beloved and notice s/he has the table manners of a barbarian, or their talk is less than the Queen's English. Your dearly beloved is no longer the paragon of everything you ever wanted in a mate. In fact, all of a sudden and without warning, you're beginning to feel that things are not as perfect in paradise as you thought. Just because you're finding out that the Epitome of Perfection is anything *but,* you also begin to ask yourself if this is really love or if you've been kidding yourself all along.

Being enmeshed in a romantic tug-of-war often happens. The change from acting like a teenager with a first crush to swiftly, irrationally wondering what you ever saw in that creep in the first place is not an uncommon phenomenon. It happens to the best of us, and sometimes even in the midst of the best relationships. Leave it to Freud to have figured this one out a long time ago. It is dear old, dated Freud who noted that having feelings of ambivalence of love and hate all at the same time is basic to human connections. Like the "Push Me/Pull You" animal in *Dr. Doolittle,* all of us at some time undergo this contradiction. Remember as a child when you wanted to become more and more independent, yet for every step you took toward growing up, you concurrently wanted to rush back to the safety of mommy and daddy? Now that we're "grown-ups" we may still have these same confusing feelings when it comes to romance.

Ambivalence sometimes has a beneficial side-effect— although one we don't often recognize or accept. That is, sometimes we have to mark (like the growing child who wants freedom and parental protection all at the same time), the boundary where our "self" leaves off and the other person begins. We've spent years growing up, maturing, accepting responsibility and decision-making and all of a sudden the person we've fallen in love with represents an infringement on our individuality. We have to pull away (however briefly), in order to reorient our-selves.

Sometimes we find ourselves disliking our partners for another odd reason: We wake up one morning feeling out of kilter with the world, grumpy, and thus reject our part-ners just because we don't like ourselves too much at the time. When you don't like yourself, it's impossible to like anyone else. So you turn your internal frustration and an-ger outward and guess who gets the brunt of it? The per-son you've been in love with for the last week, month, year, decade. This, too, shall pass. And if it doesn't, in this instance, the problem is within you—and can be changed by time, self-scrutiny and, perhaps, counselling.

Love is rarely equal at all times. We all have times when one of us needs the other more—or less. Most times, these times of see-sawing are but temporary and can be waited out. Balance will be achieved again.

Unfair and yet all too typical is the circumstance when we are angry with someone or something *outside* our rela-tionship. And again, guess who often gets to bear the brunt of this anger? You feel you cannot direct that anger at the exact person or real cause of it, so you take it out on your partner. So many of us have been trained to be polite, thus making us unable to give vent to the person who's causing our sad and angry feelings in the first place. You only hurt the one you love is a trite but true saying. And one that happens quite often. After all, you're a lot safer (or so you think) sounding off at your partner for leaving the cap off the toothpaste than you are in leveling with your boss who passed you over for a promotion.

One of the greatest breeding grounds (no pun intended) for ambivalent feelings is the bedroom. If you're not hap-py with your partner, that anger and hostility and ambigu-ity often manifests itself in bed —if it didn't start there in the first place. It's also true that outside problems (such as finances, job problems, etc.) can often be a most unwel-come and dissention-causing third partner in the bed-room.

No matter what the cause, it's always good to remem-ber that feeling ambivalent about your partner is a natural course of events over the term of a relationship. Conflicts between the two of you—whether directly related to your relationship or external—will in some way or another always end up manifesting themselves in how you feel about your partner. A good, strong, deep relationship will survive the ups and downs.

Ambivalence is a two-way street. Sometimes you'll be the one who's uncertain, at other times (and without cause on your part, that you know for sure), you'll be the brunt of ambiguity. Learning to tolerate and cope with each other's mood swings is important in maintaining any relationship. The wisest lovers of all remember that love isn't smooth, easy and always roses and candlelight. Loving relationships can endure these passing tribulations, like the flu.

Ultimatums

Single men and women more than any other social group encounter ultimatums in their personal lives. But familiarity does not assure success. The issuance of an ultimatum by a lover is serious business. And for singles it can spring the boobytrap on scores of both conscious and subconscious problems.

On a global level, ultimatums are rarely used. Diplomats know the inherent risks involved: misused or inaccurately received, ultimatums can cause war. The same is true for a man and woman in a love-relationship. There are risks, but if properly executed an ultimatum can cut through a web of and uncertainties result in a deeper experience for both.

125

An ultimatum is a final demand. Final is the key word. An ultimatum cannot become repetitious or it will lose power and significance. The person who gives another an ultimatum must be very certain that the desired goal is worth the possible consequences: departure of the loved one, loss or reduction of sex, a strained atmosphere, or a counter-ultimatum that will be difficult to handle. Think finality. Is an ultimatum really necessary?

Finding an effective ultimatum is a very creative enterprise. Think about it well in advance of execution, the pros and cons, the goal (it should usually be limited to a single desired result), the after-effects, and the likely responses. Some examples follow:

"I love you, Janet, and I believe we have a great future together, and it's for this reason that I must insist you stop dating other men."

"Why? My God, I can't believe this! I can't believe this is coming from you!"

"Well, it is. I mean it. It's very important to me."

"To *you!* Well, it's important to me that I continue seeing my friends—it just happens that some of them are male. I don't have sex with them, you know."

"No, I don't know."

"Oh, boy, you're threatened—you are!"

"Hell, no, Bethie, I won't cut back on drinking. You knew how much I drank when we first got together."

"But, Jack, it's beginning to affect you sexually."

"The hell it is . . ."

"It *is.* I know better than anyone."

"Bull—tell you what, baby, take me or leave me, just the way I am."

"I've always been possessive—I can't help it."

"Well, you'd better start helping it . . ."

126

"Have you seen a lawyer about your divorce from that woman yet?"

"No."

"Why? You promised last week."

Responses to ultimatums will vary, of course. Plan them as if you were writing a drama. Drama, to some degree, is certain to occur.

Create a time and a setting for the ultimatum. To gain maximum advantage for your ultimatum, establish what you sense is the best time and place. You know your partner, you know the best setting. But there are tips that will help.

Ultimatums between lovers have the most impact when sex is not immediately involved. Love-play is not a good time, neither is a certain period of time right after sexual encounter. Your partner might think the ultimatum is only a device to veil the real problem—his or her sexual inadequacies, which will put the person on the defensive.

An expensive candlelight dinner is probably not the time or place for ultimatums either, but the opposite was true for a young Bridgeport, Connecticut, woman. Her lover took the day off work and labored over an extraordinary dinner. When she arrived home, the table was set, candles were lighted, a good wine was waiting. This was the setting he had created for his ultimatum: he wanted her to stop her daily phone calls to her former husband. And the moment he chose was right after their first sip of wine.

"At first I was filled with anger," the young woman reports. "But then I thought how sweet and considerate it was of him to go to so much trouble. I knew he loved me. And I knew what he demanded was very important to our relationship. So, I agreed. Immediately. We had a superb dinner together, and it was the best I ever had."

A semi-businesslike setting is best, one where both parties, especially the one to whom the ultimatum is directed, are comfortable: his place, her place. Distractions should be avoided. This is important; treat it that way.

Signals that an ultimatum is coming. There are thousands.

"I'm being evicted."

"My rent's been raised—can two live as cheaply
    as one?"

"Called you today but you weren't there. And I
    really needed you."

"Oh, how I love to wake up with you next to me."

"Good sex needs continuity."

"We must have a good talk about the future. Not
    now, I'm not in the mood. But soon, darling. Okay?"

"I get the feeling that you're not where I am. Just
    where do you think we should be at this point—as a
    couple, I mean?"

"Let's pool our incomes. Then we could afford
    more fun things, like a ski trip right now."

"I'm not sleeping well . . . so restless. I'm just so,
    oh, I don't know, maybe uncertain about us."

Most ultimatums cause immediate reactions in the other party—usually negative at the beginning of the communication. A sensitive button has been pushed: a privileged territory, whether real or emotional, has been threatened, or a lifestyle has met a challenge. Now a decision must be made and the future looms ahead.

What are the options for the person who has received an ultimatum? How should he or she respond?

Don't. Not immediately. There is something about an ultimatum that wants immediacy, but do not give in to the impulse. Consider what has been said; mentally re-run the pronouncement, even repeat the words aloud. Control yourself. And *think.* Try to be objective. Estimate what compliance would mean, how rejection would change your life, and whether or not the ultimatum would work to your advantage.

Sometimes an ultimatum addresses something about you that you have always wanted to correct, and all you needed was incentive. Then, this is it . . . go for it. Unfortunately, most ultimatums are not so easy to deal with. Consider options, alternatives, and—if you have them and they're valid, not the product of hurt and hostility—ultimatums of your own. Here are some ideas about responding.

Time: "That's interesting, I'll think about it for a day or two then we'll discuss it."

Counter-ultimatum: "I'm glad you brought this up; I'd like to see you change, too."

A bargain: "I'll really try to do as you ask but I want you to do something for me, too."

Acceptance: "All right, I'll do it, but let's go over it right now so there will be no misunderstandings between us."

Rejection: "I can't go along with that, and let me tell you why. Maybe we can compromise."

Remember, whatever the ultimatum, however distressing the subject may be, time will benefit both parties . . . and your ability to think, be objective, and stay calm.

Younger people tend to issue more ultimatums; women tend to issue more ultimatums than men do. But whatever the sex or age, the ultimatum experience is traumatic for both parties. Whatever position you have in an ultimatum situation, try to keep the trauma level at a minimum.

Avoid threats and counterthreats, hold back bitterness, calm budding hysteria, and try to perceive the moment as a positive opportunity for making a relationship better or for ending it, if that is most beneficial to each partner.

The post-ultimatum period is a very special time for lovers. If the matter has been resolved successfully, there comes a period of extra tenderness, better communication, deeper love, and stronger hope for the future. And if the experience is unsuccessful, at least there has been a learning process from which knowledge has been gained, perhaps the kind that will enhance the next relationship right from the beginning.

As painful and stress-filled as ultimatums are, they send an absolute signal to men and women involved in relationships. Whatever factors are involved, there is one thing certain: The person who issues an ultimatum wants a change.

When You Know It's Over - But You Don't Know Why

It hits with the unexpected fury of a tornado. One perfectly clear, sunny day in the course of your relationship with another, the person you've been dating, living with or married to stuns you with the announcement that it's *over*. You had no warning, no hints, no advance signals that there was anything mildly wrong, much less so drastically asunder that your affair comes to an abrupt halt. You're left feeling confused, stunned, surprised and hurt. What went wrong? When did it start deteriorating? Why didn't you sense this in advance? The most painful and humiliating aspect of all is when you're suddenly jilted and offered no explanation whatsoever as to the cause of the other person's change of heart. Sometimes, the termination is halted so abruptly that not only are you left wondering what happened, but your calls and requests for a *reason* for the end are unreturned, shunned, ignored.

In this instance, you feel you're entitled to an explanation, a post-love affair outline of why the end came so suddenly and unexpectedly. You need the satisfaction of knowing something in order to cope with your grief and hurt. Surely it is the decent thing for the person who's terminated the relationship to give you five minutes of his or her time to write or call to let you know why this unilateral decision was made. Courtesy, however, is not always part of the dating scene—although it should be. Some people are so insensitive they don't even realize they should have the decency to tell you it's over. Others, the majority, are simply too "chicken" to confront you with their decision and so leave you hanging and miserable.

Even when the relationship has been more than casual, when two people have been seeing each other with some regularity and perhaps even somewhat seriously, the rejection can still be as unexpected. When clearly established relationships have already been formed, the degree of hurt is more profound and the "jilted" partner's need for an explanation is even greater.

Even in this era when women are freer to take the initiative in asking for dates and making plans, it seems that men may be more likely to abruptly terminate a relationship without explanation.

The reasons a partner may have for calling it quits vary. Sometimes it is simply because of a general restlessness or vague dissatisfaction with the situation. At other times, it may well be because he or she has started to see someone else with whom a deeper bond is formed.

Fear is, however, the most frequent cause of breaking up. *Fear of Becoming Involved,* that is. This is when one party senses that the other is becoming too serious; then he or she will probably quickly split. Sadly, a prevalent attitude today is that "getting serious" means a loss of identity and freedom; that being in love is weak. As soon as such people imagine cages are being erected, they will vanish.

And then there are some men and women who, for reasons of ego gratification need multiple relationships. The more they date, the more they salve their egos.

Whatever the reason, none are so compelling that the relationship should be severed without explanation. No matter *why* one has opted to terminate a relationship, the terminating partner should always offer some reason for the decision. It is unkind to do otherwise. So let your partner down gently, helping him or her to "save face" and retain self-respect.

A word of caution, however. Under no circumstances should you lead the other person on by offering false hope ("I'll be in touch," or "I'll call you soon."). Once you've made your decision to call it quits, then say so in no uncertain terms.

But if it happens that *you* are the one who's been dropped without explanation, just remember—anyone that insensitive and immature doesn't deserve you. It's better to be alone than in bad company.

Getting Involved With A Younger Man

Mary is thirty and her live-in lover, Scott, is twenty. She has three kids, ages five, seven, and nine. The relationship is Scott's first serious one but Mary has been married and divorced and has been involved with many different men. Is she using him? Is she "robbing the cradle" by having a relationship with a man ten years younger? Or are they both cheating each other out of love by the virtue of ten years' difference in age?

"The biggest difference I see between Scott and me is experience," says Mary. "When the littlest things go wrong, Scott falls apart. After going through a divorce and trying to support three kids for a few years, burning the toast in the morning just isn't a real big deal. When

Scott complains about little things, I wish I could tell him, 'I hope that's the worst thing that ever happens to you'."

Many women who are involved with younger men complain about their mate's lack of experience and responsibility. "Younger men just aren't interested in paying the phone bill or making the car payments," says Mary. "They'd rather spend money on immediate enjoyment like going out to dinner or a movie."

And in public or with friends, a couple whose age difference spans ten years or more are made to feel uncomfortable by the negative feelings of others. "Although our age difference is not obvious, I sometimes catch a disapproving glance from someone in public. I was really worried about what his parents would think of me, a thirty-year-old divorcee with three kids, getting involved with their twenty-year-old son. I'm less than ten years younger than Scott's mother," Mary says.

Many women cite their higher salaries as awkward points in their relationships with younger men. Older women, who have had more time to develop their positions in their careers, earn more money than their younger mates and may be accustomed to expensive restaurants and gifts which younger men cannot afford.

Perhaps one of the biggest problems in a relationship with a younger man is the sense of insecurity felt by the woman. Younger men are less future-oriented than older women and the women may find their mates' lack of concern about a long-term relationship frustrating. "He was satisfied to enjoy our relationship on a day-to-day basis," says Beth of Jack, eight years her junior. "He never wanted to make a commitment and remained unattached for our entire relationship."

Another cause for insecurity in this type of relationship is the nagging question of "What will it look like ten years from now?" The older woman frequently wonders if her man will leave her for a younger woman when wrinkles begin to appear and the age difference becomes more trying on the relationship. Even though a relationship between a younger man and older woman seems to be ideal, there is still the possibility that the man will miss the beauty of a younger girl when his older woman starts to age.

Although the cards seem to be stacked against an older woman-younger man relationship, many say that they prefer this type of arrangement. "I'm not ready for a serious relationship right now," says Claudia, a recent divorcee, "I don't feel that I am using Mark because he doesn't want a commitment either."

Diana thinks that being involved with a younger man brings freshness to a relationship. "Wayne is twelve years younger than I am and he's not spoiled by too many broken romances. Most of the men my age (thirty-five) have already had their hearts broken so many times that they are reluctant to get involved." Getting involved with a younger man has many disadvantages but several unique advantages. Evidence points to the possibility that a relationship with a younger man is beneficial on a "no-commitment" basis but, in the end, a long-term relationship between an older woman and younger man may lead to frustration for the woman and confusion for the man.

The Facts

THE TEN MOST COMMON REASONS WHY PEOPLE HANG ON TO RELATIONSHIPS

1. Fear of being alone. Misery loves company.

2. Fear that you will not meet anyone of quality.

3. Laziness. You do not want to be inconvenienced by having to force yourself to go out looking for someone.

4. You do not want to admit that perhaps you wasted your time.

5. Fear of how your friends, relatives, and even employers or employees will see, think, and feel about you.

6. Change is much more difficult than staying stuck. A loss of routine is threatening.

7. Lack of self-esteem and confidence in the relationship carries over into feeling inadequate and powerless to do something about the troubled relationship. Rather than feel how "bad" you are, stay in the relationship.

8. Fear that once your partner is gone, you will be stuck feeling empty and unable to start fresh.

9. The singles scene is tough, and you do not want to go through the whole thing all over again. It takes so much time to establish an intimate and committed relationship.

10. Fear of failure next time around.

THE SEVEN MOST IMPORTANT THINGS IN A RELATIONSHIP

For Men
1. Sex
2. Meeting mutual needs
3. Similarity of attitudes and beliefs
4. Helping each other
5. Love
6. Physical attractiveness
7. Money

For Women
1. Love
2. Meeting mutual needs
3. Similarity of attitudes and beliefs
4. Helping each other
5. Sex
6. Physical attractiveness
7. Money

WHAT ARE THE ODDS ON HOW LONG THE FIRST AFFAIR WILL LAST?

Getting through the first year seems difficult enough, but after three years, first affairs are likely to go bad.

THE ODDS: AGAINST

Age difference	WM	BM	WF	BF
3 months or less	5.3—1	7.3—1	10.0—1	32.3—1
4—11 months	3.2—1	3.5—1	4.6—1	3.5—1
1—3 years	1.6—1	1.1—1	1.4—1	1.1—1
4—5 years	9.0—1	8.1—1	4.9—1	3.8—1
More than 5 years	7.3—1	11.5—1	6.1—1	15.7—1

WM = white male
BM = black male

WF = white female
BF = black female

WHAT ARE THE ODDS ON THE NUMBER OF YEAR DIFFERENCES IN AGE IN AN AFFAIR?

The best overall chance for compatability seems to demand a partner who is one to five years older or younger. But one thing's for sure: it you and your lover are the same age, the odds are decidedly against the affair working.

THE ODDS: AGAINST

Age difference	WM	BM	WF	BF
0	19.0—1	9.0—1	9.0—1	23.3—1
1—2 years	3.5—1	3.0—1	3.3—1	2.2—1
3—5 years	3.8—1	3.0—1	2.0—1	4.3—1
6—10 years	3.3—1	4.0—1	4.3—1	2.6—1
10+ years	2.6—1	4.0—1	5.3—1	4.3—1

WM = white male
BM = black male
WF = white female
BF = black female

WHAT ARE THE ODDS THAT YOU WOULD MARRY SOMEONE OLDER OR YOUNGER THAN YOU ARE?

While one out of two husbands is up to four years older than his spouse, there are more husbands younger than their wives (14.4 percent) than there are those that are the same age (12.1 percent).

THE ODDS: AGAINST

Husband's age	
10+ years older	12.8—1
5—9 years older	5.1—1
3—4 years older	4.9—1
1-2 years older	3.8—1
Same age	9.0—1
Younger	6.9—1

V

Sex

Can We Just Be Friends?

What do you want in a friend? Make a list. Include everything you like about your present friends as well as the characteristics they don't have. The more you know about what you want, the more likely it is that you'll find it.

Don't censor the list. No one's going to see it but you. If there are certain characteristics you know you have a hard time dealing with, no matter how superficial, put them in. Be honest with yourself. Otherwise you'll never get what you really need.

How do you meet people? Don't be shy. Easier said than done, but the more you try, the easier it gets. Even if your initial attempts aren't totally successful, you'll learn not to take the rejection personally, and you'll start picking people more suited to yourself. Remember what's on your list.

Conversation is easier than you think. It doesn't have to be snappy banter. Simply saying Hi and telling the person your name can work well. A good follow-up question is anything about work—what do you do? How did you get started in that field?

A comment or question about the event you're at, whether a party (How do you know the host?), the gym (How long have you been working out?), the grocery store (How can you tell if a grapefruit is ripe?) will get you rolling. But avoid yes-or-no questions like the plague.

Just don't be negative about yourself. You're worthy. Just ask any of your present friends. After all, you're just looking to make some new ones. Plus, if you concentrate on the people you're meeting, you'll take your mind off of your own insecurities. Just be genuine. Take a real interest in the new person you're talking to and chances are, you'll be on your way to a new friendship.

Chances are the people you're meeting will be just as nervous as you are, worrying about the impression they're making on you. It's only natural. That's the way the ego works. First you think of yourself. Unless you're some kind of saint, in which case, move on to the next chapter because you probably already have all the platonic friends in the world.

How can you keep it platonic? It used to be much more difficult to have a platonic friendship. When men's and women's roles were more distinct, it was hard to imagine why you would want or need to be friends with someone of the opposite sex. Remember Gidget and Moondoggie?

Thankfully, times have changed. Women have found that men can be sensitive (sometimes even more than women) and men have found that it's no crime to have feelings. Or talk about them.

So it would seem, the first step in keeping it platonic would be to talk about it. Unless, of course, there is absolutely no physical attraction between the two of you. Get the feelings out first, because it'll never work unless both people are in agreement about what the relationship is and isn't. And what you want is a confidante, not hurt feelings later.

Your present sweetie also has to be in agreement. If that person can't be convinced that your new buddy is simply that, your new buddy won't be around for long. That, or your sweetie may not be around for long. Luckily, more and more couples are realizing the value of outside friends. One person can't fulfill every need. And don't think that viewpoint isn't important. Sometimes that can be your biggest help in working out other kinds of relationships. Once you have a close platonic friend, you've got a sounding board. So maybe the next time someone of the opposite sex tells you they want to be "just friends," you'll be flattered rather than feel rejected.

Remember, friendship takes time, whether with the same or opposite sex. Give it the time it needs to grow. Let it proceed at its own pace. Like any kind of relationship, you can expect too much too soon, and end up disillusioned and disappointed. Keep in mind that your new friend has a life apart from yours. Don't dump too much of yourself on him or her too soon. But at the same time, don't be afraid to let the real you show through.

Given half a chance, you'll have a new friend who can accept you for yourself. Given enough new friends, you'll have a support network that'll see you through anything life may dish out. And that's the best reason to be just friends.

Reading The Sexual Signals

You are out on a date with someone you are very attracted to. The evening has gone well: The wine was delightful, the conversation never stopped, and those jokes of yours really *were* funny. But what next? Should you make a move? There are many clues in your companion's attitude and actions, and by tuning in to them you can figure out if you both want to take things a step further.

CLUES

Consider that person's physical demeanor when standing and when moving. Does the person appear comfortable with his or her body? Are movements tight, relaxed, or openly sexual? Does the person have what is called a "sex center"? (Pia Zadora does.) An "ego center"? (Charlton Heston and William Shatner do.) A "superego center"? (Pope John Paul II does.)

How do the person's clothes accentuate the appearance? Are the right bulges accented and the wrong ones minimized? What do the clothes indicate about the person's sense of taste and trend? Do they seem to be making a statement about relative conservatism or liberalism?

Do you find yourself discussing best flicks at the French Film Festival? the Erotic Film Festival? or prize heifers at the Midwest Feed and Grain Expo?

Does the conversation come around to sex? Does he or she remain natural? Or go out of the way to avoid it? Or include it?

Does he or she seem to seek or to avoid your touch?

How does it feel to hold hands? Comfortable? Exciting? Does he or she seem playful, or does the hand lay there like a dead fish?

Does he or she take advantage of an unsuspecting moment to touch your ear, your hair, or something else? Does the person's touch seem to convey sensitivity, intensity, and sensuality? Platonic friendship? Brute strength? Does it indicate experience and pleasure at the touch of the opposite sex?

Try to make eye contact, what does that seem to tell you?

Shshhh...
Sex And The Single Parent

How does one lead a fulfilling personal life without worrying about the children? Sex is not easy for the single parent; it is a touchy subject that must be taken seriously to avoid hurting everyone involved: parent, lover, and children.

Children are very sensitive: The addition of a new person into the home can alter the child's behavior somewhat, but even more so if the child is not being dealt with honestly and tactfully. There is not one clear-cut case that carefully outlines the how-to's and the wherefore's in dealing with sex and our children because each situation demands an individual approach, but there are certain things to keep in mind when you want to begin a new sexual relationship with someone.

Honesty seems to be most important. Your children will most likely give you a hard time, either by putting instant demands on the new "mommy" or "daddy," or being so angry with you that they set up failure for your new relationship. Let them know that you have needs, and that you also have limits to which you will tolerate their anger. Talk about it, keep it in the open, and empathize with your children. If they feel you understand, they will probably begin to accept the outsider.

Honesty about the fact that you are a sexual person will not damage a child, but sneakiness will. And if you insist that your child not tell anyone, you will certainly instill in your child a distrust of you and a distrust of the other person. It may cause your child to wonder if sex is something to be ashamed of.

Follow your instincts, assume responsibility for yourself, and be prepared for some rocky roads to readjustment for your children. If your partner can remain open to these changes, then that adjustment will go all the smoother. The first step is up to you; after all, it is you who brought this person into the home, it is you who has those sexual needs, and it is you who must respect the child's confusion, anger, and hurt.

Sexually-Transmitted Diseases

Sexually transmitted diseases—venereal diseases— have reached epidemic proportions in this country. The reported cases of syphillis have gone up by 10 percent every year in the past decade; there are 2 million cases of gonorrhea a year and genital herpes simplex infections attack over 500,000 people annually. These figures are just the reported cases of gonorrhea (herpes simplex is not reportable). Scientists and doctors believe that at least 30 percent of all cases go unreported each year. Sexually transmitted diseases are second only to the common cold in the number of Americans they infect each year.

Despite these grim statistics, there is good news. Treatment of sexually transmitted disease (STD) has made good progress in the past few years: there are many more clinics to treat patients, the treatments are more effective, new and better treatments are coming soon, and the veil of ignorance and shame that has shrouded sufferers is rapidly lifting.

The best way to prevent STD, and the best way to handle it if you get it, is to know what it is and how it can be treated. Single people are especially vulnerable to contracting STD because of their large variety of social and sexual contacts. Arm yourself with knowledge.

The different types of disease we group together as "venereal diseases" actually have very little in common except their method of transmission—sexual contact—therefore the term "sexually transmitted diseases" is more accurate and informative. STD can be caused by bacteria, viruses, or other microorganisms. These germs thrive in an environment like the one provided by a person's genital area: warm, moist and protected. In order to infect another person, the microorganisms have to enter the body through prolonged contact with an orifice. In the past, STD primarily attacked the genital area, but now infections appear just as frequently in the anus and the mouth as these orifices become more popuar in sexual contact. Some forms of STD do not even require sexual contact. Syphilis, for example, can enter the body through an open wound. Gonorrhea is rarely transmitted through tilet seats and tissue paper, but infestations such as lice and scabies can be picked up from clothing, restrooms and bedding.

SYPHILIS

Syphilis is the most serious of all STD because it is frequently difficult to detect and can be potentially deadly if not treated.

Causes: Syphilis is caused by "spirochetes," small cork-screw shaped bacteria. These bacteria need a constantly warm, moist, environment to thrive and will die outside of the human body; therefore they need prolonged contact to spread. Syphilis bacteria can live in any orifice—the mouth, anus, or vagina—and can spread through any probing extremity—penis, tongue, even a finger.

Symptoms: After an incubation period of between nine days to three months—the time between catching the disease and manifesting the first symptoms—the small number of syphilis germs picked up during contact multiply a thousand fold. In the first stage of the disease, a small spot appears in the area of sexual contact. This spot then grows into a small, button-like sore that sometimes oozes a colorless liquid. A few weeks later the glands may swell, but this swelling is usually not noticeable.

In the second stage, the bacteria spread from the initial contact area to the entire body, either immediately after the first stage or weeks later. Once the bacteria spreads the infected person starts to have flu-like symptoms such as headache, aches and pains, fever, loss of appetite, and general malaise. The symptoms may get more severe, however, causing a dark red rash on the extremities, hair falling out, sores in the mouth, throat, nose, or genitals, and swollen glands. These second stage symptoms usually disappear, even without treatment, in three weeks to ten months.

After the second stage, the disease enters a latent period where there are no symptoms, but the bacteria are still moving throughout the body. The bacteria cease to be infectious after two years, and the latent stage can last any amount of time—from five months to fifty years.

The third stage of syphilis is the most severe, and occurs in at least a third of the people not treated earlier. The syphilis bacteria finally settle in one part of the body and gradually destroy it. They can attack the skin, ligaments, joints or bones, causing lesions and severe ulcers. The most serious damage occurs if the bacteria attack the heart, blood vessels, or nervous system, causing insanity, crippling, paralysis, or death.

Of critical importance is the very real possibility of a syphilitic mother passing the disease to her child. It is highly likely that the child would die, be crippled, or badly scarred as a result of contracting the disease.

Test and treatment. Syphilis is not always easy to diagnose because the initial symptoms are mild or indeterminate. Usually a blood test called VDRL is given to detect syphilis antibodies in the blood; if sores are present, they are tested for syphilis bacteria. A blood test called FTA will disclose whether a positive VDRL is a false or true positive. The FTA is preferred to confirm the VDRL, in doubtful cases.

Penicillin or other antibiotics are used effectively for treatment, and in the first or second stage, treatment will almost always cure the disease, although tests will be necessary two years after treatment to make sure the bacteria has been totally eliminated. In the latent or third stages, treatment can kill the bacteria and stop the disease from spreading further, but it cannot repair the damage already done.

GONORRHEA

Causes: Gonorrhea—or "The Clap"—is one of the most contagious of all venereal diseases because people carry it without knowing it. Doctors say that 90 percent of women who have gonorrhea never know they have it. But not only women are carriers: Men can have the disease asymptomatically, too.

Gonorrhea is caused by bacteria that thrive primarily in the genital area and that are transmitted almost exclusively through sexual intercourse. Gonorrhea is sometimes transmitted through oral sexual contact, and anal sexual contact can also spread the disease.

Symptoms: In men, the symptoms appear after a very short incubation period, from a week to a month. Initial reactions include discomfort inside the penis, a thick yellow-green discharge from the tip of the penis, and pain or burning during urination. The bacteria may spread to nearby areas, causing inflammation and abscesses in the urethra, tenderness and swelling in the testes, and itching and discharge from the anus. If the mouth is infected there is a soreness and swelling of the glands. If untreated, the bacteria can spread throughout the body, possibly causing arthritis in the joints and sterility.

In women, gonorrhea has a longer incubation period, and there are fewer symptoms. The initial symptoms are usually very mild: some discomfort urinating and possibly a yellowish vaginal discharge. Usually, symptoms appear after menstruation. If untreated, the bacteria may spread and cause more serious symptoms, including swollen glands, inflammation and pain in the cervix, uterus and fallopian tubes, and sterility. If the woman is pregnant, the bacteria could cause premature birth, umbilical cord inflammation, maternal fever, blindness in the child, and even death to both the fetus and mother. Gonorrhea can also result in infertility.

Test and treatment: Gonorrhea can be diagnosed by a culture of the discharge or a smear of the infected area. Treatment is by penicillin or other antibiotics, taken either in a pill form or intravenously. Tests are now being done on a gonorrhea vaccine, and the results are mildly promising.

NGU

Causes: The most common sexual diseases are those caused by a microorganism called Chlamydia Trichomonas and these diseases are commonly labeled "Nongonococcal Urethritis" (NGU) in men and "Non Specific Vaginitis" (NSV) in women. People may get NGU or NSV when their sexual habits change: they have more frequent sex, they have new partners, or after a long period of time they return to a partner who is infected.

Symptoms: In both men and women the symptoms of gonorrhea are very similar—primarily a discharge and discomfort urinating. NGU or NSV differs from gonorrhea, however, in that the incubation period is longer and the discharge is lighter in color—usually clear to milky white. If untreated, NSU or NSV may spread and cause pelvic or cervical infections in a woman and testical inflammation in men. Tests have also shown a link between chlamydial infections in mothers and eye inflammation and pneumonia in the newborn babies.

Test and treatment: Doctors usually prescribe antibiotics for men and women, in addition to advising abstinence from sex during the period of treatment. If the infection has spread, it usually takes longer to cure, and sometimes reappears months or years later. Reinfection and self-infection are highly likely.

CANDIDIASIS

Cause: An overgrowth of Candida Albicans, a yeast-like fungus that normally lives in the mouth, stomach, rectum, and vagina. This fungus does not cause problems unless it is stimulated into overabundance. This stimulation can occur from pregnancy, diabetes, and overly sweet or starchy diet, and certain drugs and contraceptives. Men can catch it from sexual relations with a woman, or just from heat and exercise. Both sexes can pick up the disease in gyms or at pools.

Symptoms: In women, the usual symptoms are an itch in the genital area, a discharge that is either thin and watery or white and thick, pain, a yeasty smell from the vagina, burning urination or intercourse, and a red swollen vulva. In men, the symptoms include itching in the genital area, painful urination, dry redness on the head of the penis, and possibly small bumps or little sacs of white cheesy matter on the penis and scrotum.

Test and treatment: A specimen of the discharge will reveal whether the symptoms are of the yeast infection or another more serious STD.

The three most commonly prescribed treatments are hystatin cream or suppositories, miconazole, and clotrimazole cream or tablets. All three treatments are applied directly to the vagina once or twice daily. For men, a cream form of the medicine is applied directly to the penis. It is advisable to avoid sex during treatment, or at least to wear a condom, and keep your genitals dry.

VENEREAL WARTS (CONDYLOMATE ACUMINATA)

Causes: Warts that appear around the penis, rectum, or vagina are transmitted by sexual contact.
Symptoms: After an incubation period of a month or more, skin colored, cauliflower-shaped eruptions occur, frequently covering the entire genital area if not treated promptly. Venereal warts can lead to cervical cancer.
Treatment: The warts must be removed in one of four ways: topical lotion and medication, liquid nitrogen, or burning with an electric needle or laser.

TRICHOMONIASIS

Causes: Tiny parasitic protozoa that infect the vagina in women and the urethra in men, either through sexual contact or via damp washcloths, towels, or bathing suits shared with an infected person.
Symptoms: The incubation period is four to twenty-eight days after exposure. The infection usually causes more discomfort in women than in men. Men may experience a mild genital itching while women may have a greenish-yellow discharge, painful urination, inflammation of the vulva, itching, and lower abdominal pain.
Treatment: The most common treatment is the medication metronidazole, administered as a pill to men and women. It's important that both parties avoid sex during the period of treatment. Do not drink alcohol when you are taking this medication.

MOLLUSCUM CONTAGIOSUM

Causes: A sexually transmitted virus.
Symptoms: Non-itching, bubble-like bumps on the genitals or inner thighs that spread fast and are very contagious.
Treatment: The bumps must be removed by a physician.

PUBIC LICE ("CRABS")

Causes: These six legged parasites, similar to body lice, live and lay eggs in the pubic hair. They can spread by sexual contact, or through towels, clothing, bedding, and toilet seats.
Symptoms: Intense itching and visible lice and eggs in the pubic hair. Sometimes the lice burrow under the skin causing tiny bumps and small spots of blood on the underwear.
Treatment: Usually a prescription lotion or cream called Kwell will kill the lice, and some over-the-counter medications and pubic shampoos are also effective. It's also important to thoroughly clean all clothing, bedding, and towels to remove all eggs and lice, and to refrain from sex during treatment.

HEPATITIS

Causes: Hepatitis, which is classified as either type A or B, is not considered strictly a STD, but each type can be sexually transmitted under some conditions. Type A, usually transmitted through food, can spread through sexual contact, especially anal-oral contact. Type B, usually transmitted through transfusion of infected blood, has also been found to be present in the saliva and semen of an infected person, therefore can be transmitted by oral sex or even prolonged kissing.

Symptoms: Jaundice is the most obvious symptom yellow-orange skin tone, a slight yellow coloring of the white of the eyes. Other symptoms include extreme fatigue, low-grade fever, orange-yellow urine and light colored stools.

Treatment: Hepatitis requires a doctor's care and sometimes even hospitalization. This is a very serious disease.

POSSIBLE SIGNS OF A SEXUALLY TRANSMITTED DISEASE:

If you have one or several of these symptoms, it's important to have a check-up by your doctor or clinic for possible VD infections.

1. Unusual discharge from penis or vagina.
2. Sores, rash or ulcer around genitals, anus or mouth.
3. Itching or soreness of penis, anus or vagina.
4. Swollen glands in groin area.
5. Pain or burning sensation on urination.

WHERE TO GET HELP

1. Family doctor, dermatologist, internist, urologist, or gynecologist. He or she will know your medical history and therefore be in good position to follow up treatment and handle any possible complications. Two drawbacks, however, are cost and possible embarrassment (if you already know the physician).

2. VD National Hotline: From anywhere in the U.S. call (800) 227 8922; from California, the number is (800) 982-5883. The hotline will give you confidential information and can refer you to clinics in your area.

3. VD clinic: You may prefer the anonymity of a clinic. Most cities have publicly funded clinics that offer free and confidential testing and treatment for VD. Clinic health workers will also notify your sexual

contacts for you if you prefer to remain anonymous. The drawbacks to a clinic are possible long waits to see a doctor, reluctance by the clinic to doing culture tests because of the expense, and the clinic's limitations to diagnose and treat.

PREVENTION

Although you can never totally avoid the possibility of contracting some form of STD, following these simple rules can help stop the disease from spreading to you.

1. Practice good hygiene: wash genitals and anal area before and after sex, especially if you don't know your partner well; don't share or swap towels, underwear, or bathing suits; be extra careful and clean in public restrooms. Always urinate after sex. Drink plenty of water or, even better, cranberry juice, to help flush your urine of bacteria.

2. Some contraceptives help: especially a condom, vaginal creams and jellies, and spermicides.

3. Get a regular medical check-up: for a single person with a variety of sexual contact this is *essential*. Have exams three or four times a year, and make sure to request specific exams for STD, even if you do not have symptoms.

4. If you get a disease, make sure it's properly and promptly cured, and religiously go to your follow-up appointments.

5. Avoid sex during treatment for a STD.

6. Know your partners. If you have a lot of casual sex partners, make sure you have a way to contact them and they can contact you.

7. If you do contract a STD, make sure all your recent contacts know—all your partners within the last six to eight months.

8. Emergency steps: if you sleep with someone who you later realize has a disease, follow these emergency measures: urinate immediately after contact

to flush out germs, wash the genital area with soap and water, or wash with Betadine douche. Women can insert contraceptive foam, cream or jelly within the vagina and on external genitals also.

9. If you are about to have sex with a casual partner, check his or her genitals first. If you see signs of a STD, refrain from sex.

The Facts

WHAT ARE THE ODDS ON FREQUENCY OF SEX AMONG SINGLES?

Almost one out of three singles (30 percent) has never had sex more than once a week. The vast majority (69 percent) have never had sex more than four times per week. At the other end of the activity scale are 13 percent who have had sex at least eight times a week. Included in this group are a hardy band (4 percent) who've had sex twenty or more times in one week, our bedroom athletes!

THE ODDS: AGAINST

Maximum frequency of sex in any one week	
1 time	2.3—1
2 times	5.3—1
3 times	6.7—1
4 times	9.0—1
5 times	15.7—1
6 times	24.0—1
7 times	13.3—1
8 times or more	6.7—1

WHAT ARE THE ODDS THAT YOU WILL HAVE SEX WITH SOMEONE TONIGHT?

Unfortunately we were only able to uncover data on this question for singles aged eighteen to twenty-four. Seventy-five percent of all single men in the group had premarital sex in the past year with a median frequency of thirty-seven times. Two-thirds of all single women have had sex in the past year. Among this group the median frequency is far higher than that of single men; just over once a week. What accounts for the difference between the two groups of singles? Married men.

THE ODDS: AGAINST

Men aged 18 to 24	11.8—1
Women aged 18 to 24	9.0—1

WHAT ARE THE ODDS THAT YOU WILL SLEEP WITH SOMEONE NEW TONIGHT?

Both single men and single women under the age of twenty-five have an average of two sexual partners a year. Between the ages of twenty-five and thirty-four that rises to four for men and three for women. But we do not know how many of these are new lovers or how many are carryovers from previous years. The odds below assume a fresh start each year.

THE ODDS: AGAINST

Men 25	181.5—1
Men 25 to 34	90.2—1
Women 25 years	181.5—1
Women 25 to 34	120.6—1

WHAT ARE THE ODDS ON THE NUMBER OF SEXUAL ENCOUNTERS IN AN AFFAIR?

Over 40 percent of women have had sex with each man they have been with at least 10 times or more, while just 6 percent have had a single sexual encounter. Roughly 1 of 4 reported the number of encounters varied widely from partner to partner.

THE ODDS: AGAINST

1 encounter	15.4—1
2—5 encounters	3.9—1
6—10 encounters	13.1—1
More than 10	1.5—1
Varied greatly from partner to partner	2.8—1

HOW DO THE ODDS ON MAXIMUM FREQUENCY OF SEX RELATE TO EDUCATION LEVEL AMONG SINGLE WOMEN?

Frequency of sex and higher learning go hand in hand. For example among women who have done some graduate work, 37 percent have at one time or another had sex five or more times in one week, versus 16 percent of those who at most finished high school.

THE ODDS: AGAINST

Maximum frequency of sex in any week	Up to completion of high school	Up to completion of college	Some graduate work
1 time	1.6—1	2.6—1	4.0—1
2 times	419—1	5.2—1	4.9—1
3 times	8.1—1	6.1—1	6.1—1
4 times	7.3—1	10.1—1	4.9—1
5 times or more	5.2—1	3.8—1	1.7—1

VI
Living Together

What Do You Call Your Roomates

Have you decided what to call that person you are living with? If you are married, it is simple. If you are not married, the answer usually involves a nervous stammer. Well, here is a list of the most common names for that very special person in your life—you know, the one you spend so much time with but for whom there is no name.

Names for women
My woman
My lady
My girlfriend
My steady woman, lady, girl
My lady friend
My old lady

Names for men
My man
My boyfriend
My good friend
My steady

Names for men or women

My friend   My mate
My good friend   My associate
My best friend   My partner
My lover (my love)   My roommate
My fiancee (that's cheating)   My companion
My sweetheart   My paramour
My valentine
The person I live with
My cohabitant
POSSLQ (person of the
opposite sex sharing
living quarters)

Financial Arrangements

BANK ACCOUNTS

Money management and financial problems have broken
up more marriages than practically any other factor.
With an unmarried couple, the strain and the financial
risks could be even greater, and the temptation to let this
problem come between you could prove overwhelming.
The surest way to avoid entanglements is to *keep your finances separate.*

No laws prevent unmarried couples from opening a
joint bank account. Banks can help you decide how many
signatures are needed to write a check or make a savings
withdrawal. You may want each person to be able to sign
for the money, or you may want to make both signatures
necessary for a withdrawal so that neither person can
withdraw all (or most) of the money from the account
without the other's knowing.

One ingenious system of banking that works for a number of couples falls right between keeping totally separate accounts and completely pooling the money: four separate checking accounts titled "yours," "mine," "ours" and "car."

All income from both individuals goes into the "ours" account. Each person has a checkbook and the money deposited is split in half between each checkbook, so that even if one person spends all of his or her allowance the account will not be overdrawn (unless both of you lose self-control). If either book runs too low, temporary transfers can be made. At the end of the month, the books are balanced and the joint bank statement reconciled. The ours account pays for all the living expenses the two of you decide to share—rent, food, utilities, and the like.

Once a month a modest amount is transferred from the ours account to each individual account (yours and mine). This money is each person's personal allowance, to be spent on clothes and other discretionary items. Neither person has to account for the money in the personal account.

The car account can stop a lot of potential headaches. Car maintenance is usually one of the major expenses in any household, and a separate car account will help you monitor those expenses and perhaps save money by discouraging excessive driving. Keep a record of the number of miles driven and make deposits of thirty cents (or other agreed sum) per mile into the car account from the ours account. This covers all operating expenses, and includes fifteen cents a mile for depreciation. This amount will probably go up, depending on the increased maintenance and cost of gas. You could also set aside some car money into a savings account for purchasing a new car in the future.

Try to keep a required minimum balance in each account to avoid service charges that could add up to quite a sum with four accounts.

Charge Accounts and Credit Cards. Today most stores and banks will issue credit cards for single or joint accounts as long as each person has a good credit rating, steady income and pays debts. Occasionally, unmarried couples have difficulty opening joint charge accounts because some creditors feel that such a relationship is not stable and therefore they might not pay up. Do not pretend you are married in order to get a joint charge account because this could constitute fraud and get you in a lot of trouble. Almost all stores, even those that do not issue joint cards, will allow other people to sign on one person's card. This can serve many of the same purposes as a joint card, except that the one person to whom the card is issued is responsible for all the debts.

Unless you simply must have joint accounts, an unmarried couple is much better off with separate charge cards and credit. With a joint account both parties are legally responsible for all debts on the account, which could get troublesome if you break up, or if one of you had difficulty restraining his or her spending impulses, or if one of you has a history of bad debts. By keeping your accounts and finances separate you protect yourself against creditors who may be chasing your partner. You are not legally responsible for the debts of someone you are living with, and creditors cannot attach your property to pay someone else's debts, unless you have merged your finances.

Beware of cosigning anyone's loan or credit application. A person who cosigns a loan promises to pay the entire amount in the event the person actually receiving the loan cannot or will not pay. If the primary debtor defaults on payments, the creditors may come after the co-signer-signer for payment, and if the cosigner refuses to pay the creditors can sue and garnish the cosigner's wages to pay the debt. Therefore, never cosign any loan unless you are fully capable and willing to pay it off. One runs less risk of loss by being a guarantor than a cosigner because many states require that the creditor obtain a judgment before attempting to collect from the guarantor.

A store or lending institution is not required to lend to anyone. Approval of credit depends upon whether the company considers you a good or poor financial risk, and each company arrives at that decision by different means.

In 1977 Congress passed the "Equal Credit Opportunity Act" making it unlawful for creditors to discriminate on the basis of "race, color, religion, national origin, sex, marital status or age, or because all or part of a person's income derives from any public assistance program." Most creditors interpret "marital status" to mean only either single or married, thereby allowing them to deny credit to unmarried couples. At this time, there are no court decisions challenging that interpretation.

Many credit companies research an applicant's credit history through credit bureaus that specialize in keeping extensive credit files on individuals. Creditors and other sources contribute information to these bureaus so that other prospective creditors can contact the agency and obtain the information for a fee. Most credit bureaus claim that their records only contain data on past paying performance and that they do not cross-index unmarried persons living together, but this may not be true. Frequently, people discover personal information unrelated to credit in their files, and find out that the bad credit rating of their live-in partner has filtered over into their file. Under the Federal Fair Credit Reporting Act, you have the right to go to a credit bureau to review your file, although they may charge a fee. You also have the right to correct false information and to put comments on your file to explain your point of view if you believe it is inaccurate or a wrong impression is being given. The credit bureaus do have the right to reasonably limit the length of your comments.

HOUSING

Renting and subletting. If you thought it was difficult finding a place while you were a single person, you may find it even more difficult as an unmarried couple. Ideally, landlords only care if you pay your rent on time, do not damage the apartment, and do not disturb the neighbors, but some landlords may equate an unmarried couple with instability, or may simply object to that lifestyle on moral grounds. At the present time there are no federal laws barring discrimination against unmarried couples, so your rights depend on the laws in the state, county, or city in which you live. Most local areas have no laws barring this kind of discrimination, and if you live in a state where cohabitation is illegal, landlords are well within their rights refusing to rent to you. And local laws may allow such discrimination even if cohabitation is legal.

If you live in an area where the laws do not protect you against discrimination, here are a few practical tips. Do not flaunt the fact that you are not married. If they assume you are, do not *volunteer* information to the contrary (but do not make any false statements if asked directly). Many large apartment buildings these days are run by corporations; you may never see the owner but will rent through an agent. Try to find apartments in areas that are more socially liberal, near universities or urban centers, for example. Be on your best behavior whenever you meet the landlord, and emphasize your good financial and personal references.

Do not rent from someone who obviously disapproves of an unmarried lifestyle. You may slip past him the first time, but if he finds out he may feel irritated that you tried to deceive him. The apartment is probably not worth the potential hassle.

Unmarried couples living together should make a written agreement between themselves as to how payment of the rent is being divided, when it must be paid, who pays for utilities and telephone, and other charges, what happens if one person wants to move out, becomes unemployed, and so on. But remember, any agreement you reach will only be binding between the two of you and will not affect the landlord or other creditors.

If one person moves into the other person's house or apartment, be sure to check the lease or rental agreement to see how many people are allowed to live on the premises and what the restrictions are. Many leases limit occupancy to the lessor and members of the lessor's immediate family; lovers are usually not considered immediate family. Although you may be able to slide by without telling your landlord that a new person has moved in, it is better to inform the landlord in writing of your plans. He may allow it, with perhaps a slight increase in rent. If you have a rental agreement, the landlord may be able to evict you, except in areas where discrimination against unmarried couples is illegal or under many "tenant favored" rent-control ordinances. With a lease, there is a better chance he will allow it, as long as you tell him in advance, although he may not renew your lease when it expires. Research the laws in your area before moving in together, and make contingency plans to find another apartment.

If you simply move into your friend's apartment, you have no obligation to pay the rent, nor do you have any rights of a legitimate tenant, including taking over the apartment if your friend leaves. If you want to become a tenant, you can sign a new lease or rental agreement that specifically includes you as tenant, or make a verbal agreement with the landlord (a written agreement is better).

When you move into a friend's apartment, you should write an agreement between you specifying who pays how much of the rent and bills, to what extent each of you is obligated to the landlord, and what happens if either of you wants to move out. If you get into a serious dispute and you have no written agreement, here are a few guidelines. The person whose name is on the lease has first claim on the apartment, especially if he or she lived there first. The other person should be given a reasonable amount of time to find a new place. If both names are on the lease and you both pay rent to the landlord, your claims on the apartment are probably equal. Talk out the situation, or get an impartial third party to arbitrate between you. Never lock up another person's belongings. Do not deny a person access to his or her home. Unless the person has no legal right to live there (does not pay rent, has not signed a lease), locking someone out is illegal and you could be sued for damages.

Buying. A homeowner and real estate agent will have no compunctions about selling a house to an unmarried couple—they just want the money. The banks and the financial institutions to which you will apply for a loan are a different matter. All financial institutions consider two factors in deciding whether or not to loan money or real property: the value of the property itself and the personal financial circumstances of the borrower.

It has been very difficult for unmarried couples to get loans. Most banks and financial institutions consider an unmarried couple to be very unstable, therefore they will not lend money jointly. They will usually insist that only one person's name be on the loan, the person with the highest income. This closed-mindedness has been lessening a little in the past few years, but do not expect a bank to welcome you with open arms. If you are lucky enough to get a loan in both names, always remember that both of you are legally liable for the entire debt. In case of a default on payments, the bank can foreclose on the property and pursue one or both parties for repayment. Also remember that if you sell the house to a third party, you continue to be responsible for the mortgage until the bank agrees to release you from your obligation and lets the other party assume the mortgage. Check if your mortgage has a pre-payment penalty.

In most states, there are three ways to take title to a house: *sole ownership, joint tenancy,* and *tenants in common.*

If the foreclosure sale brings a price less than what is still owed on the home, some state laws allow the bank to pursue one or both parties for repayment of any deficiency. Other states (for example, California) have "anti-deficiency" legislation that precludes the bank from going after the parties and only allows the bank to retain the sale proceeds.

Sole ownership means that the person whose name appears on the deed is the sole owner of the property, and your partner legally has no claim on the house, even if he or she made house payments. Joint tenancy means that the two (or more) people who sign the deed share in property ownership, have the right to use the entire property and, most importantly, if one person dies the other joint tenant(s) automatically takes title of the deceased person's share without probate, even if there is a will to the contrary. Tenants in common means the same as joint tenancy *without* the right of survivorship. That is, if one party dies, his share goes to his estate to be divided according to his will; it does not automatically go to the other party.

Because jointly purchasing a house is a serious responsibility, it is almost essential that you draft a contract between you that answers the following questions:

If one person moves into a house already owned by the other, what legal agreements can be made to protect both of you?

If one person invests more money in the house than the other, what legal agreements can be made to protect both of you?

If a person's share of the house payments are compensated by other services, such as housework, how will this compensation be expressed?

If you split up, who keeps the house?

Is the other party to be reimbursed to any degree for his or her contributions toward the home (perhaps half of the amount of reduction of the principal balance of the loan)?

What means are used to decide who keeps the house if both of you would like to keep it?

How do you decide the value of the house if you split up?

If one person keeps the house and buys the other out, how is this transfer made?

It is also a good idea to take your draft of your agreement to your lawyer to check the legal practicalities and to make sure the agreement says what you intend it to say.

EMPLOYMENT

As far as your employer is concerned, you are "single." Do not volunteer any personal information while employed or while looking for a job. A company's only concern about your living arrangement should be its implication for your stability and dependability as an employee, and for fringe benefits. A person interviewing you for a job has no need for information beyond "single or married?" and he or she legally cannot ask for any more details. Most employers these days do not care about the private life of an employee unless it is flaunted, but if an employer finds out about your living arrangement and objects, threatening you with dismissal, there may not be much you can legally do about it. In many states, private employers are free to hire and fire people just as an employee is free to resign, although this is changing all over the country. Definite exceptions to this principle are public service jobs and companies that explicitly declare they do not discriminate on the basis of whom employees live with.

In most public service jobs you probably will not get in trouble living together unless you are an educator. Primary and secondary level teachers who cohabit are targets for dismissal for "immoral behavior," especially in conservative areas. Be discreet and keep a low profile.

TAXES

Unmarried couples cannot file joint tax returns. Unmarried individuals usually claim "single" status, although in certain cases they may file as "head of a household." To be eligible for the latter, however, you must have a dependent who is a child, relative, or in-law. The filing status of a married person can be "married filing jointly," "married filing separately," or "head of a household." Your eligibility for filing status is outlined in the Internal Revenue Service's tax instruction booklet.

A rule of thumb is that if two persons who are living together earn approximately the same amount, there is probably a tax disadvantage if the two people marry, although recent tax legislation has somewhat reduced this "marriage tax." On the other hand, if two persons living together have incomes that are vastly different, there is probably a tax advantage if the two marry. This advantage can be increased if the person with the lower income has dependents. In any event, it is not a good idea to pass yourself off to the IRS as married if you are not. They may not find out, but if they do the penalties will be exorbitant.

INSURANCE

It used to be nearly impossible for unmarried couples to get life insurance because companies did not believe that one partner had an "insurable interest" in the other. The person you name as your beneficiary (the person who gets the money when you die) no longer has to have an "insurable interest" on your life. If a company refuses, go somewhere else. Do not lie to them and say you are married because if you try to collect the company may legally refuse to pay on the grounds that you defrauded them. For every company that will not sell to you, there are five that will. Be careful though, some companies may charge higher rates for unmarried couples.

Homeowners' insurance and renter's insurance are now much easier to get for unmarried couples. Sometimes, a company will not write a joint policy for the two of you but will make you sign two separate policies, at a higher rate, of course. If this happens, go somewhere else. An insurance broker who is sympathetic to your situation can help you find a good policy.

Unmarried couples who want to purchase separate automobile insurance will have no problem, but if they own one or more cars jointly, it may be difficult to get the coverage you want. Many companies will not insure both people and both cars in the same way they would if you were married; instead, they will try to issue you two separate policies listing one of you as primary driver and the other as secondary for each car. If you have two jointly owned cars, you are not entitled to this. It is best to find a sympathetic insurance broker to help you out.

WILLS

When you die, your estate is distributed by one of two ways: according to your written will or according to the laws of "intestate succession." (Intestate means without a will.) All states have specific rules of succession to determine who inherits from you if you do not make out a will. According to the rules of intestate succession in all fifty states (except in those states that recognize common law marriages), an unmarried couple relationship *does not exist*. Therefore if your partner dies you are not entitled to *anything* unless stated specifically in your partner's will or unless you purchased property under a joint tenancy contract, in which case there is nothing in the estate to be taken.

In order to protect your property and your inheritance intentions, you should first make out a property ownership agreement with your partner that lists who owns which items and then draft a will that specifies how your estate is to be divided. You should get a lawyer's assistance in making out a will because in some states handwritten wills (called "holographic wills") are not valid, and in all states probate laws are monsters that will feed on any little mistake or irregularity in your will.

Living-Together Contract

"Why do we need a contract?" you may ask. "Didn't we decide to live together so we could avoid paperwork, formalities, and courts?" True, you probably did. But there are very good reasons why you and your partner should write a contract between you. First, face the facts: In today's world, it is practically impossible to avoid litigation, and even if you try, litigations usually find you anyway. So be prepared. Secondly, no body of law exists to determine the exact legal responsibilities of unmarried couples. Only recently have such relationships been acknowledged by the courts as legitimate partnerships, and decisions handed down in these cases are not universally applicable: The cases are decided after reviewing very specific circumstances that are unique to that case, and any general conclusions that the court expounds are too general to be of much practical use. The contract married couples automatically receive from the state is very precise and the result of years of regulations, court decisions, and legislation—unmarried couples have no such contract, yet they have at least as many, if not more, legal responsibilities and expectations as a married couple. Without a written agreement that covers financial and legal obligations, any disputes between unmarried people would have to go to court, and the case would probably become even more complicated, drawn-out, and messy than a divorce! If you have a contract, that dispute

173

may never happen, and if it does, it will be a lot easier to resolve.

So you agree that you need living-together contracts, but the word "contract" frightens you. Your mind conjures up images of astronomical lawyer's fees and pages of fine print that bears only a passing resemblance to English. Relax. A contract is just an agreement between two people to do something, or not to do something. Most contracts that you have encountered in your life, and the living-together contract, are merely your written promise to do something in exchange for someone else's promise to do something else. For example, you promise to pay your rent in exchange for your landlord's promise to let you live in his building. Anyone can make a contract, and it will be perfectly legal as long as the promises in the contract are legal and they were not made under duress. Your living-together contract only needs to be clearly written, specific, and inclusive to be valid.

What do you put in your contract? Anything you want, that is the beauty of it: how you will pay your rent, who owns the television, who pays the gas bill, who does the dishes, who gets the house if you separate, and so on. Legally, the courts can only enforce agreements pertaining to personal property and real property (land, houses, apartment leases): they cannot pass judgment on who should do the dishes. But that should not stop you from putting it in, because putting down all your personal agreements and mutual responsibilities will give you the security of knowing that any disagreements you may have can be resolved a little more objectively.

There are three steps to drawing up a living-together contract: making your agreement, structuring the contract, and writing it down. Once you make your agreement, the other two steps are easy. You should take time to discuss all the economic and personal considerations in your living arrangement, and work out the best compromise between you. In general, if you *both* feel like you are giving in a little more than the other person, then you have reached a good compromise. With regard to personal and real property, a cohabiting couple usually has much more freedom to decide how it can be divided between them than a married couple (unless the married couple makes up a special contract). The state community property laws make the decision for married couples, but unmarried couples make the decisions for themselves. The design of the contract depends on what you discover to be important in your living agreement. Typically, living-together contracts can emphasize property division, jointly acquired items, joint projects, homemaking services, household expenses, personal needs, financial support, handling of finances, or any combination of these. Once you have reached your agreement, know what you are going to say, and know the structure to put it in, writing the contract becomes a breeze.

You certainly do not have to get a lawyer's help in drafting a contract, but if your considerations seem rather complex, or if a substantial real property value is involved, you may want to take your contract to a lawyer for a review. Many law firms, legal clinics, and counselors are familiar with the special needs of unmarried couples, and some lawyers have already drafted and printed standardized contracts. You start with these and make additions or deletions to suit your specific needs.

The simplest and most inclusive agreement an unmarried couple can make is a waiver of all financial claims on each other. The waiver should clearly state that:

Neither of you has an implicit obligation to support the other.
Neither of you intends sharing your earnings or property with the other.

Any property acquired while you are living together belongs to whoever paid for it, or belongs to each person comnensurate with their contribution.

Any future agreements to share property or earnings must be in writing.

Neither of you expects compensation for any services rendered to the other.

175

Guide For Drafting A Living-Together Contract

Compile this information and answer a few preliminary questions before you begin to draft your contract.

   I. **Marital status of each person**
  II. **Names, addresses, and telephone numbers of present or former spouses or parties**
 III. **Children of each person**
     A. Names
     B. Sex
     C. Birthdates
     D. Birthplaces
     E. Identity of natural parents
 IV. **Employment of parties**
     A. Occupation of parties
     B. Names and addresses of employers
     C. Income from employment
     D. Income from other sources

V. Health of parties
  A. Medical conditions requiring attention
  B. Health insurance plans and options
    1. Joint policy
    2. Separate policies
  C. Life insurance plans
VI. What is nature of your living arrangement?
  A. Cohabitation without marriage
    1. With children
    2. Without children
  B. Cohabitation with possibility of marriage
  C. Sharing of housing and facilities as roommates
  D. Sharing of income
    1. Equal sharing of all earnings during relationship
    2. Partial sharing of earnings and other income
    3. No sharing of income
  E. Sharing of expenses
    1. Equal sharing of expenses
    2. Sharing of expenses in proportion to income
    3. Sharing of expenses in proportion to use of facilities
    4. Apportioning certain expenses to each person
    5. Other sharing arrangement
  F. How do you plan to share property?
    1. Joint and equal ownership of all property acquired during relationship
    2. Joint and equal ownership of only certain specified property or types of property acquired during relationship
    3. Joint ownership of property in proportion to each person's contribution to the purchase price
    4. Separate ownership of property, with each person merely sharing use during relationship
    5. Separate ownership of property with a rental arrangement for use by one party
  G. Sharing of child support obligation
VII. List the property of parties
  A. Separately owned property
    1. Property owned before nonmarital relationship

2. Property acquired during nonmarital relationship by
    a. Gift
    b. Bequest
    c. Gift by will (also called "devise")
    d. Inheritance by descent
3. Property acquired with separately owned property
4. Earnings of each person and the property acquired from those earnings

B. Jointly owned property
1. Property earned during the nonmarital relationship where each person agrees that such property will be jointly owned
    a. Property earned by either or both partners
    b. All of such property, a stated percentage or in proportion to earnings
2. Property acquired from earnings where each person so agrees
3. Residence
    a. To be purchased jointly by both people
    b. To be conveyed by one party to both of the parties to hold as tenants in common

C. Obligations
1. Debts and liabilities occurring before the nonmarital relationship may be treated as the individual responsibility of the person who incurred those debts and liabilities
2. Debts and obligations incurred during the relationship:
    a. May be shared equally
    b. May be shared equally or allocated between the two persons depending on the type of debt or liability (Remember that this allocation is only binding between yourselves and does not affect any rights the creditor may have.)

Once you have this information, use the following guide to help you draft a nonmarital contract. Answering the questions will give you a rough outline. Then draft your own contract and ask your lawyer to review it, if you like.

I. Support

A. Will one person be financially supporting the other?

B. If so, is the support for life? Or

C. 1. Until the death of either person?

2. Until marriage of either person?

3. Until the cohabitation of supported person with another person?

4. Until termination of the nonmarital agreement?

D. Is the support of one party only for a specified length of time, for example, only to provide educational expenses? Is the support to be reimbursed in whole or part at some later date?

E. Is the financial support of one person in exchange for services rendered, (homemaker, construction, etc.)?

F. How will the children of the nonmarital relationship be supported?

1. Each parent must furnish the necessary clothing, food, shelter, and medical attention for his or her own child

2. Each parent must also support and educate his or her own child according to such parent's circumstances

3. Will the contractual duty to support be terminated on the supported child's

a. Death?

b. Majority?

c. Marriage?

d. Emancipation?

(State laws often provide that child-support obligations end on one or all of the above, unless the child is unable to care for himself.)

4. What arrangement will be made for the support of any existing child(ren) of one person by a former relationship?

II. Property

A. Will the property owned by one person before the nonmarital relationship remain separate property?

B. Will the real property owned by one person before the nonmarital relationship

    1. Be conveyed to the parties to jointly hold as tenants in common?

    2. Be rented to the other party?

    3. Be shared freely without contribution by the other?

C. Will the property acquired during the nonmarital relationship remain separate property? This property could be

    1. The earnings of one person

    2. Acquired by the earnings of one person

    3. Acquired with separate property

    4. Acquired by gift, bequest, gift by will or inheritance by will

D. Will the property acquired during the nonmarital relationship become jointly owned property?

    1. Property acquired through the earnings of either or both of the individuals

    2. Property acquired through separate earnings during the relationship

    3. Property acquired through the transference of the residence of one person to both individuals as tenants in common or as joint tenants at the time of the execution of the nonmarital agreement

E. Will the separately owned property be comingled with jointly owned property? (If so, it may lose its separate character unless it can be specifically traced.)

III. Living accommodations

A. If the residence is owned by one person at the time of the execution of the nonmarital agreement, is it to be

    1. Conveyed to and held by both people as tenants in common?

    2. Or, rented to one party by the other during the relationship?

    3. Shared freely without contribution?

B. If the residence will be rented or leased by both people:

    1. Will they rent or lease from a third-person lessor?

    2. Or, will one person rent the residence and sublet the premises to the other person?

C. Will one person make financial contributions from his or her separate property in order to maintain the household?

IV. Miscellaneous

A. How will the agreement be terminated?

    1. On the written consent of the parties?

    2. On the marriage of either of the individuals?

    3. On written notice?

B. On termination of the agreement, how will jointly owned property be divided?

C. On termination of the agreement, how will jointly owned property be appraised?

D. Will there be life insurance on the life of the party providing support?

E. Will there be insurance to protect the personal property of each person?

F. Will both people agree to make mutual wills (that is, name each other as beneficiary)?

G. How will household expenses be divided?

H. What agreement will be made as to sharing of household responsibilities?

I. What kind of agreement will be made covering joint projects?

V. Documents that may need to be prepared depending upon your agreement

A. A deed by which the residence owned by one person at the time of the execution of the agreement is to be conveyed to both of the parties as tenants in common or as joint tenants and used as their primary residence during the course of the nonmarital relationship

B. A last will and testament

C. A lease or sublease agreement respecting the residence of the couple

    1. If the couple is to lease from a third person, they must execute a lease agreement as lessees

2. If one party is to lease the residence to the other, the owning party must execute an agreement as lessor and the other party will be the lessee

3. If one person is leasing the residence from a third person, present lessee must execute a sublease agreement with the second person of the nonmarital agreement. The original lease may require the landlord's consent to any sublease.

VI. Other procedures

A. Arrange for preparation of a life insurance policy

1. On the life of the supporting person

2. In the amount and in accordance with other terms stated in non- marital agreement

3. In which the supported person is named as the irrevocable beneficiary, or revocable beneficiary upon termination of the relationship by means other than death

B. Designate an appraiser and an alternative appraiser of property and notify them as to their responsibilities in relation to the terms of the nonmarital agreement

VII

Single
Again

Breaking Up

It's over. Or it is so close to being over that your relationship might as well have a tombstone prepared for it. Even when the couple is still together physically (in the same house, still dating, whatever) there are those times when it feels as though you are just going through the motions.

When dealing with a relationship that is not sailing as smoothly as it once was, sometimes one has to let go. But letting go need not be tragic: Even the most obsessed among us should find the promise of new adventure and renewed promises a consolation.

The two most common errors people make when relationships stop working is that they let go too soon, or they hang on too long. If you still get some joy from the relationship and if you find that the good things you derive from the relationship outweigh the pain and suffering and boredom — which may only be temporary — then by all means, stick with it!

If going together has become a bit boring and that is the reason you are thinking of ending the relationship, you might be well advised to hang on a bit longer. First, we all go through phases of waxing and waning passions—and sometimes both partners' interests wane at the same time.

At other times, we become too lackadaisical. When was the last time you splurged on some sexy underwear? Or planned a trip out of town for the weekend at a romantic, secluded hotel? Or spent a few hours at a hot tub club? Or bought flowers, lit candles, and shared a bubble bath instead of just hopping into the sack as usual?

Every couple argues sometimes. However, if you begin to notice that all your arguments are about the same thing, or that past transgressions (real or imagined) are all the other person wants to argue about, then you need a good soul-searching series of talks. Better still, find a counselor who will work with both of you until you can once and for all say goodbye to all those past sore spots.

But sometimes we stop trying when we have used up every available iota of energy on a relationship that seems to be going nowhere. We feel that we have already lost, so there is no use going on. We may feel neglected, abandoned, abused, frustrated, ignored. You may also have lost all respect and regard for your partner. The relationship is just not worth fighting for any more. In these cases, it certainly seems logical to call it quits. Other times, you simply stop trying because you meet someone else who seems to offer you a better chance for happiness.

There may be cause to throw water on whatever embers may still be smouldering if you finally realize the person you are with is inappropriate for you. Maybe a character trait or fault you overlooked or refused to acknowledge in the first flush of romance is really unbearable and irreconcilable with who you are. Or maybe, as sometimes sadly happens, one partner simply stops growing or becomes totally insensitive.

Why continue in a relationship that does not seem to be worth it? Making the decision is a struggle—and one of the hardest decisions you will probably ever have to make. You may still have some lingering tenderness and good feelings for your partner and having to end this relationship will be akin to being the one to decide whether or not to pull the life-support systems on a loved one. If you and your partner are miserable, or if you are both unwilling to put any positive energy into this relationship, it does not have to continue. When love has gone one way and you another, there is only one answer: termination.

How Long Does It Take To Recover

Just how long does it take to recover? What can you do to help speed the healing process? No one can accurately predict when grieving will end and renewed determination to try again start. Some people—most in fact—take a few months to recover emotionally from a break-up. In the meantime, they may mope and fret and try to escape (either by totally altering their lifestyles and patterns, or throwing themselves into their work or other passions so that they have little or no time left to feel sad). Others take years to really "get over" a love affair. Sure, they have an affair or numerous love affairs in between, but in the back of their mind and in the most hidden part of their hearts, there's always the tender longing for the original partner.

An interesting case of a love affair that never quite ended involved Sarah and Brett. They dated for four years

187

during high school, then broke up after graduation because Sarah wanted to get married right away, and Brett felt he had to finish law school before he could do so. Both married on the rebound within the year. Both chose spouses so very much like the other that it seemed each was living out a fantasy through loving someone else as replacements. They never contacted each other for twenty years after high school graduation, but had knowledge of each other's whereabouts and activities and mates and children via their families, who still kept in touch casually. Then one day Sarah, who was divorced, wrote to Brett, sending him a picture of their senior prom that she had unearthed while moving.

Several weeks later, Brett replied in a very warm but casual tone that he had recently re-married but that he was very, very glad to be in touch with Sarah again. Several months later, Sarah awoke to a call from Brett (their first contact in twenty years) asking her to join him in Hawaii for a week of sunning, surfing, and snorkling. She hesitated for all of five seconds (it taking that long for her to wrestle with her conscience about his being married) and agreed. Their reunion was one of which heavenly dreams are made. Their love had never really died despite the years of separation, the other spouses, the divergent interests and accomplishments. They vowed to resume their love affair as soon as Brett could get divorced. This took a few years, during which time the two maintained a low profile so Sarah could avoid feeling trapped in an "other-woman" role. After a quarter of a century, Sarah and Brett were married. They will probably surf off into the sunset together a la *On Golden Pond.*

In other cases, the fantasies one holds about a long lost lover are buried quickly and forever when a chance or planned reunion takes place. Then you may discover that the object of your fancy is not a dream reincarnated, but rather anything but.

No matter which one jilts the other, the pain that ensues can be more than you bargained for. Sometimes we hope the other, more reluctant partner will mellow and change with time. When they don't, it takes strength and courage to call it quits. In this instance, you simply have to come to terms with the fact that the relationship isn't working and never will and call a halt to it. Depression may follow and if it seems that coping with this pain is more than you can handle by yourself (even with your best efforts of keeping active, opening yourself up to new experiences and new relationships, etc.), then therapy may be the answer.

A bit of trivia: experts contend that women recuperate faster from a break-up than men do.

Whatever you do, it is okay to wallow in self-pity for a while and it's acceptable to turn to friends for support and empathy. However, dwelling on the hardships of breaking up is ultimately self-destructive and can turn your friends off, so be sure to look for support in appropriate places.

Tips For The Newly Single

Your re-entry into singlehood may be relatively simple or more like the re-entry of a spacecraft into the atmosphere, fiery and scary. Whatever the circumstances, adjustment of some kind is involved. Most psychologists would agree that the major obstacle in adapting to widowhood, divorce, or separation is our adjustment to being alone for the first time in a long time. The difficulty stems from the fear that somehow something is wrong with us, that we are not worthy or desirable. The following tips may ease you into a positive and healthy readjustment to your new identity.

Recognize that you need a period of adjustment. Do not give yourself a deadline for readjustment because everybody's time clock is different in different circumstances. Understand that time is a very important healing agent, and believe that the scars of loss will mend. It may help to make yourself a list of areas in your life that are, and will be, changing. This will not only ensure fewer surprises but will also provide you with a specific plan for putting yourself together.

Recognize your needs and wants. There are a multitude of approaches to this, but the goals are usually to help you get out of the house, to revitalize dormant hobbies, and to indulge yourself in new and positive experiences. Many churches and community organizations sponsor support groups; hearing about other people's problems can make you feel less alone and can give you ideas about helping yourself.

Let your friends and relatives know that you are available when you feel that you are ready to be. If they try to introduce you to people before you are ready, thank them for trying but be honest and say that you are just not ready to take that step. Be careful not to burden friends and family with details of all your woes and experiences, but keep them up to date on how you are feeling and let them know you need them so you can get the valuable support they give freely.

Try to deal with all of your feelings about your former relationship. Unresolved, bottled-up residual feelings will leave a bitter taste unless you wash them away. Talk to people who have had a similar experience, or join a group, or look into therapy. You will feel better for it.

Do special things for yourself. For example, make a special meal with some nice wine, rewarding yourself for being alone. Think of it as being "with yourself" instead of "by yourself."

Remember your health. New lifestyle patterns can directly affect your well-being. According to two sociologists at St. John's University in New York, individuals who have just terminated a relationship are highly susceptible to colds, flu, viruses, headaches, and fatigue. They also found that the sickly single places the blame for his physical state on his ex-partner, on the new romantic interest (if there is one), or on the fact that he may have entered a relationship too soon.

Try not to get deeply involved for at least six months. Carefully consider the ramifications of getting involved in a commitment. Are your wounds healed? Unresolved feelings about your ex could only be a detriment to a new relationship. It is interesting to note that two-thirds of divorced women and slightly less than two-thirds of divorced men remarry within the first five years after a divorce, usually for life. Difficulties in the second marriage generally occur because the marriage took place too soon after the break-up, before the individual came to terms with his or her autonomy.

If you do get involved again soon after ending a relationship, remember that your new partner is a completely different person. You will not necessarily have the same problems and unmet needs. You do not need to hang on to unhealthy habits or repeat your performance in the last relationship. Instead, use the previous relationship as a learning experience from which to solidfy your new one.

Two axioms. These may be the most important. Learn to say no. And do not forget how to laugh.

No one said that the adjustment would be easy. Keep in mind, however, that there are many single people who are happy and satisfied. It is a viable lifestyle option in which you can discover the benefits of independence and pilot your life in the direction that suits you, be it as a single or as a couple.

Twelve Ways People Handle Rejection

The singles dance is an established American institution. Because of its prominence, several studies have been made of dance hall behavior. One study revealed that if you are rejected at a singles dance, you will probably react in one of twelve ways.

Controlling visibility. Hide. Do not let anyone else know you have been rejected. Go into a corner or behind a barrier or into a dark room.

Withdrawal. Walk away. If you have been refused, walk out of the place, either physically or psychologically.

Avoidance. Don't try. Avoid asking someone to dance and you avoid getting rejected.

Limiting involvement. I'm not part of this. If rejected, refuse to associate or attach yourself to the activities or the importance of the activities at the dance.

Self-enhancement. You're okay. Tell yourself that even though you were rejected, you are still a worthwhile person.

One-downing others. You're not okay. Put others down, be aloof and inaccessible. Discredit others; try to reject them before they can reject you.

Ridicule others while projecting an air of social distance and superiority.

Redefinition. Talk it away. Redefine the rejection so that it was not a rejection in the first place.

Denial. I don't believe it! Refuse to believe that you were rejected.

Internalization. I deserved it. When you internalize, you do not feel you deserve anything but rejection.

Repair damaged self-esteem. Am I really that bad? Talk the situation out with a friend and seek solace from that friend, or ask the friend to help you redefine the situation.

Change the self. I'm not that person anymore. Change or plan to change your personality so you will not be rejected again.

Humorous response. Laugh it off. See the rejection as part of a humorous game or skit in which you are one of the participants.

Saying Goodbye To The Bye-Bye Blues

This section deals with the reason you're single in the first place—the break-up—and all the loving things you can do for yourself to get you through this difficult and frustrating time.

It's been demonstrated that when a relationship ends, people go through many of the emotional stages that mourners do. First there's disbelief, where you're simply numb, going through the motions, sometimes a little unconsciously. Chances are you can't eat, you can't sleep, you can't concentrate—if you were at the beginning of the relationship, we'd call it love or infatuation. At the end, we call it depression.

Next is denial. You can't believe this is happening to you. You expect the object of your affections to walk through the door and tell you that it was all a big joke and you can go back to life as usual again.

And when you stop denying, anger surfaces. "How dare he? How could she leave?" Sometimes you turn this anger inward. "How could I let this happen? What kind of stupid, short-sighted, unlovable, person am I?" Remember, you wouldn't be human if you weren't angry now. The person you loved, trusted, relied on has left, and that abandonment hurts. So give in to the anger: scream. Give yourself fifteen good minutes all by yourself. Let it all out. Take all that anger, frustration, resentment and vocalize it, good and loud. Then say, "I've done that," and move on. If those feelings resurface, do it again. Don't let it fester inside you. It will only make you more resentful and more likely to turn your anger inward.

If you can't scream, get physical. Get a punching bag, or take a self-defense course and learn to release the anger and protect yourself at the same time. Go running or join a gym; you'll let off steam along with the sweat. And you'll end up in better shape emotionally and physically.

Make a list of all the things you're angry at. Each time you reach a standstill, ask yourself, "Is there anything else about this that makes me mad?" When you can't think of anything else, look closely at the list. Somewhere in there is the most important reason for your anger: that's the one to work on.

Rationalization is the stage when you try to figure out why. It is also the stage where you're most apt to try the patience of your family and friends. Much as they want to help, they may find it difficult to hear you continually rehash your relationship. So try to maintain your perspective and talk about sports, politics, what's going on in *their* lives every now and again. You will find yourself more and more able to put it out of your mind.

There are some things you can do for yourself at this stage. Re-enact a recent argument aloud, playing both parts yourself. A tape recorder will help a lot. If you're honest, you will really gain insight when you listen to what you were saying. Were you fighting fairly, or just venting anger? And your partner? Did you feel better when the fight was over, or did it just feed your anger? Was the argument about something trivial to mask the real problems?

Then think about how you would handle that argument now. How would you fight about that same subject? What would you say? Pretend to tell that person what you feel. Then take the other side and defend it to yourself. You may find some of those "what if's" disappearing when you do this.

Rather than idealizing the situation, make a list of all of the qualities you want in a mate, then compare your ex. How does he or she measure up? Is it that you were expecting more than anyone could possibly be? Or did you settle for less than you really could be happy with?

Right now, the best relationship you can build is one with yourself. So treat yourself to something wonderful, something that's maybe a bit of a luxury: stay in bed with a box of chocolates and a good book all day; don't answer the phone; get a professional massage; take a weekend trip, even if it's just to the little motel on the other side of town. You'll feel like you've gotten away and that'll do you a world of good. The trick is to do something solely for yourself. Not because anyone wants you to do it, but because it's something you want to do. If you don't think you deserve a little pampering, make a list of everything you've done for everyone else recently and then see if maybe you can't do just one nice thing for yourself in return.

The final stage is your acceptance of your new status as a single person. This may be your first time on your own, making your own choices, independent of what other people want or need you to do. Taking the next step is very scary, and many people do one of two things: get involved in a protective relationship almost immediately, so they still have someone else to make the decisions; or they retreat from the world. Neither improves your self-worth or helps your independence.

What can help are goals. Set yourself some short-term and long-term goals: big goals like career changes, small goals like writing letters. You need all kinds of goals because as you start achieving those goals and crossing them off your list, you will experience a real sense of accomplishment.

If you want to lose weight, find a healthy diet you feel you can follow and throw yourself into it. Having control over one part of your life will make it easier to get control over other parts. And you'll feel better about yourself as your image in the mirror improves.

Keep busy. Get involved in group activities that will

keep your mind and body occupied. Join a gym, bridge group, charity organization. Take lessons in something you have always wanted to learn. Singing. Tap dancing. Pottery making. Who knows, you may even meet some new people. And if you don't, at least you have found yet another place where you belong.

How To Reject With Kindness

Hate to say goodbye? Stay in relationships too long? Accept too many dates with people you don't want to see? Knowing how and when to say goodbye—as easily and painlessly as possible—is a skill. It takes practice, and an understanding of what rejection really means.

There are fifty-nine million single American adults. Bells don't ring every time two of them meet. But society places so much emphasis on finding the ideal mate that you often lose track not only of *what* you are doing but *why* you are doing it. The why is crucial. You're not engaged in the dating jungle to suffer purposely. Dating—or a relationship—is supposed to bring pleasure into your life. You want to spend time with an attractive member of the opposite sex whose chemistry clicks with yours. What about those whose chemistry does not mesh with yours?

First, you can eliminate some grief by closely screening potential dates. If you are being fixed up, get as much information as possible from the go-between. Also, examine the go-between's motives. Is he or she trustworthy—or a former friend seeking revenge?

The telephone is an effective means of pre-screening. Ask a lot of questions. Try to get a sense of the other person. Is he or she a heavy drug user, terminally unemployed, or ravenously sex-oriented? If so, and if you object, cancel the date, or arrange to meet just for a drink—for not more than half an hour.

Successful screening calls can elicit surprisingly personal data.

He: You didn't mention kids. Do you have any?
She: No. Not yet.
He: You obviously want them.
She: Yes, I'd like a family.
He: I can't have kids. I've been "fixed."
She: Well, it's not necessary I start my family in the next three weeks.

Still, the woman decided not to accept the first date. Children were high on her life agenda; at thirty-five, she felt she had no time to spare.

But even with pre-date investigation, instincts can fail and you can find yourself sharing coffee and life's pleasantries with the wrong person.

Sometimes there's a specific moment when you know a relationship is doomed.

He: You certainly seem to have a lot of friends.
She: Oh, I do. I don't know how I'd exist without my "hug net work."

For this male, "hug network" reminded him of the narcissistic 70's and sent shivers up his spine. He knew irreconcilable differences existed.

After you realize that a potential relationship is not going anywhere for you, you need to communicate that fact to the other person. In some cases, it's clear that neither of you wants to continue seeing the other, and verbalizing the obvious is unnecessary. But that's not most instances.

So what do you say and when do you say it? Some people choose the road of least resistance: equivocation. Giving a mixed message to someone you don't like, but who would clearly like to see you again is fine—if you're a fan of cowardly, unjust, and ultimately self-defeating behavior. People are resilient; they can accept reality. It's the ambivalent half-promise that is debilitating.

Sometimes your date will initiate a decision by asking, "Can I call you?" or "Can we see each other again?" If the moment is opportune, you can immediately proceed with your farewell. If you're timid or tongue-tied—or if you prefer a less personal confrontation via Ma Bell—postpone your rejection. Instead, "call me" or "I'll call you" will suffice, and you can then decide what you want to say.

A basic guideline for rejecting is this: be concise, direct, and kind. Start with something positive and reasonably sincere, such as "I've really enjoyed spending time with you. You seem like a bright, caring person with a lot to offer. However . . ." But keep your "however" statement short! Stick to:

"I don't think this would work."
"We'd never get along."
"We're just too different."

Your real reasons are irrelevant. It doesn't matter if they're rational or justified. You've made a decision, and you owe no one, not even yourself, an explanation. And you don't owe the other person a thorough analysis. It's even arrogant to think your rejection will make any long-term difference. Respect the other person—assume that he or she can handle rejection.

One San Francisco woman in her twenties had an intense, long-standing crush on a man in her office. He finally asked her out, and she thought they enjoyed being together. At the end of the evening, he brought her to her door.   Before she could invite him in, he said, "I had a

very nice time tonight, but I won't be calling you again."
The woman was distressed.

When she awoke the next morning, however, she felt differently. She said, "I was disappointed, but there was a certain freedom in knowing that he wasn't going to call. It was really a mature way of behaving." Thus, what may seem abrupt is actually kind.

Sometimes you need only impose a temporary restraining order. You like the other person but need to ward off premature physical advances.

"Let's wait."
"This part has to proceed slowly."
"I prefer to get to know a person first."

You will probably invent your own appropriate or favorite line. Some people prefer humor. "I'm sorry, but my sister (or brother or therapist) insists that I go out with someone at least five times before we fool around."

People can get pushy and manipulative. A friend had the following confrontation with a photographer she met at a party. After a subsequent dinner date, he made a play for the bedroom.

He: I like you. You're the first person I've liked in years.
She: Thanks. I like you too, but we're not getting intimate.
He: Ever?
She: I don't know about ever. I just know about tonight.
He: Yeah, but I might not meet anyone like you for years.
She: That's right. You might not.
He: But what about my feelings? Don't I have anything to say about this?
She: You've already said it.

The evening ended shortly thereafter, and she never saw him or his photographs again.

Some people persist until they evoke anger or rudeness.

She: Why won't it work?

He: It just won't.

She: But why? What's wrong with me?

He: Nothing's wrong with you.

She: Then why can't we see each other again?

He: Because, at least for me, I don't see a future to this relationship.

She: But you've hardly given it a chance. I mean, all we've done is spend an hour over coffee together.

He: I know.

She: Is it the way I look? Aren't you attracted to me?

He: You're attractive.

She: Then why can't we see each other again?

He: Because. Because it's just not there.

And then, other people put themselves into situations in which they know they will be rejected.

One woman answered a newspaper ad describing herself as 5'5" and 125 pounds. A man responded, and after a lengthy, upbeat phone conversation, they agreed to meet the following evening for a drink. The woman appeared—5' and 225 pounds. The male politely pretended that nothing catastrophic had occurred. At the end of the date, the woman asked, "Will we see each other again?"

"I don't think so," the man answered.

"Why not? Because of my weight?"

"No, because there are major differences between us."

"What do you mean?"

"I mean, you're not open and honest. You lied in your letter."

"How else could I get someone to go out with me?"

The woman knew she would be rejected. She set herself up. Afterward, she could console herself with the thought, "Aren't men terrible? They won't go out with me because I'm fat." She could instead answer ads which specify larger women, or decide to lose some weight.

Most people, however, are not persistent whiners or professional rejectees. They're simply looking for the same thing you are—and will respect you for your honesty and directness if you decide not to see them again.

To Date Or Not To Date

Being single is often associated with wild living. A constant round of dating. Romance city. And anyone who's spent any time single, knows "it ain't necessarily so."

In fact, sometimes singles choose not to date. There are any number of circumstances that make dating a fate worse than death. When you've been really burned in a romance, for example, chances are, you're feeling less than favorable toward the opposite sex. Bitter might be a better description. Dating is definitely not recommended at this time. Or maybe you've been on a social merry-go-round. Feeling a bit dizzy? Get off the ride and give yourself a chance to recharge your emotional batteries. Or maybe the pressure you feel isn't romance related. Work or school is taking its toll. Don't add to the pressure with a new relationship. You'll only feel more drained and you could even resent the object of your supposed affections.

Illness is a good reason not to date. Not the sick and tired of the dating scene kind of sick, but actual physical illness. Particularly if you're contagious. There's also emotional unwellness, too. That can take a few forms, depression, for one. Sometimes, when you're depressed, you only want to be around people who'll readily understand your situation and can accept you as you are, no matter how you're behaving. Dating doesn't seem to make much sense.

Sometimes you just plain want to be alone. It might be because you want to rediscover who you are, because you are reassessing life goals or because you want to devote your time to something creative, or maybe because you like the feeling of independence that being alone provides. It's at this point that your friends and family may be most vigilant about getting you into the social scene. "What do you mean you want to (go to the movies, spend Sunday, insert your own choice of activities) alone? It's unheard of. It's unspeakable. It's un-American." Don't cave in to the pressure if you don't want to date. Your family and friends will forgive you one day, even if today they don't understand.

TEN COMMONLY STATED REASONS FOR BREAKING UP

1. "We've grown apart." (or changed, or, you have changed)
2. "I'm interested in someone else."
3. "You cheated on me."
4. "I don't know."
5. "We have different sex drives (interest)."
6. "We can't talk about anything anymore."
7. "You bore me."
8. "We just end up fighting."
9. "We are interested in different things (career interests)."
10. "Our families don't get along."

THE TEN GREATEST EXIT LINES, AND THEN SOME . . .

1. "Goodbye"
2. "I've got to get home to: (a) take care of my kids"
                              (b) feed my dog/cat/ gerbil/goldfish"
                              (c) let in the plumber"

3. "I've got to leave town for several weeks/months/years. I'll call you when I return."
4. "An old friend came back into my life."
5. "I'm looking for a permanent relationship, and you're not it."
6. "I'll call you."
7. "We're just too different."
8. "I really enjoyed the evening. Thank you."
9. "Let me take your number and I'll call you."
10. "You're an interesting person. I'll call you."
11. "I'll be out of town for some time. I'll call you."
12. "I think we're on different wavelengths."
13. "The 'X Factor' just isn't there."
14. "Let's face it. It's over."

SUBJECT INDEX

THE SINGLES ALMANAC
QUESTIONNAIRE

Dear Reader:

I want to take the time to thank you for reading this edition of THE SINGLES ALMANAC. I hope that you find it useful. I would like to know what subjects you would like to learn more about. If you hear about some service experience or opportunity for singles, please fill out the questionnaire below and send it to the address provided.

SEND THIS QUESTIONNAIRE TO:

THE SINGLES ALMANAC
c/o Great Expectations
11050 Santa Monica Boulevard
Suite 100
Los Angeles, CA 90025-3595

NAME:_____

ADDRESS:_____

CITY:_____ STATE:_____ ZIP:_____

SEX:_____ AGE:_____ MARITAL STATUS?_____

OCCUPATION:_____

1. Have you ever been married? _____

2. If yes, how many times? _____

3. Do you hesitate going out in your free time unless you can be with a friend_____ or a date? _____

4. What activities do you enjoy doing as a single person?
_____

5. Would you enjoy these activities as much or more if you were able to share them with someone else?

_____

6. Does your work environment permit you to meet enough available quality single people?_____

_____

7. Although you may be meeting a lot of single people, are you not meeting the right quality of single people?

_____

8. Would you like to find a special relationship and get married? _____

9. Do you enjoy dating a number of people without wanting to commit myself to a long relationship?

_____

_____

10. What are the most difficult aspects of being single?

_____

_____

_____

11. Where did you learn of THE SINGLES ALMANAC?

_____

12. Where did you buy THE SINGLES ALMANAC? _____

_____

13. Please use the following area to give us suggestions on sections of this book which were most helpful to you, and on activities or opportunities you would like to see included in future editions. _____

_____

_____

_____

World Almanac Publications
Order Form

Quantity	ISBN	Title/Author	Unit Price	Total
	31655-X	Abracadabra! Magic and Other Tricks/Lewis	$5.95/$7.95 in Canada	
	32836-1	Africa Review 1986/Green	$24.95/$33.95 in Canada	
	32834-5	Asia & Pacific Review 1986/Green	$24.95/$33.95 in Canada	
	32632-6	Ask Shagg™/Guren	$4.95/$6.50 in Canada	
	32189-8	Big Book of Kids' Lists, The/Choron	$8.95/$11.95 in Canada	
	31033-0	Civil War Almanac, The/Bowman	$10.95/$14.75 in Canada	
	31503-0	Collector's Guide to New England, The/Bowles and Bowles	$7.95/$10.95 in Canada	
	31651-7	Complete Dr. Salk: An A-to-Z Guide to Raising Your Child, The/Salk	$8.95/$11.50 in Canada	
	32662-8	Confidence Quotient: 10 Steps to Conquer Self-Doubt, The/ Gellman and Gage	$7.95/$10.75 in Canada	
	32627-X	Cut Your Own Taxes and Save 1986/Metz and Kess	$3.95	
	31628-2	Dieter's Almanac, The/Berland	$7.95/$10.25 in Canada	
	32835-3	Europe Review 1986/Green	$24.95/$33.95 in Canada	
	32190-1	Fire! Prevention: Protection: Escape/Cantor	$3.95/$4.95 in Canada	
	32192-8	For the Record: Women in Sports/Markel and Brooks	$8.95/$11.95 in Canada	
	32624-5	How I Photograph Wildlife and Nature/Rue	$9.95/$13.50 in Canada	
	31709-2	How to Talk Money/Crowe	$7.95/$10.25 in Canada	
	32629-6	I Do: How to Choose Your Mate and Have a Happy Marriage/ Eysenck and Kelly	$8.95	
	32660-1	Kids' World Almanac of Records and Facts, The/ McLoone-Basta and Siegel	$4.95	
	32837-X	Latin America & Caribbean Review 1986/Green	$24.95/$33.95 in Canada	
	32838-8	Middle East Review 1986/Green	$24.95/$33.95 in Canada	
	31652-5	Moonlighting with Your Personal Computer/Waxman	$7.95/$10.75 in Canada	
	32193-6	National Directory of Addresses and Telephone Numbers ,The/Sites	$24.95/$33.95 in Canada	
	31034-9	Omni Future Almanac, The/Weil	$8.95/$11.95 in Canada	
	32623-7	Pop Sixties: A Personal and Irreverent Guide, The/Edelstein	$8.95/$11.95 in Canada	
	32624-5	Singles Almanac, The/Ullman	$8.95/$11.95 in Canada	
	31492-1	Social Security and You: What's New, What's True/Kingson	$2.95	
	0-915106-19-1	Synopsis of the Law of Libel and the Right of Privacy/Sanford	$1.95	
		Twentieth Century: An Almanac, The/Ferrell		
	31708-4	Hardcover	$24.95/$33.95 in Canada	
	32630-X	Paperback	$12.95/$17.50 in Canada	
	32631-8	Vietnam War: An Almanac, The/Bowman	$24.95/$33.95 in Canada	
	32188-X	Where to Sell Anything and Everything/Hyman	$8.95/$11.95 in Canada	
	32659-8	World Almanac` & Book of Facts 1986, The/Lane	$5.95/$6.95 in Canada	
	32661-X	World Almanac Book of Inventions`, The/Giscard d'Estaing	$10.95/$14.75 in Canada	
	29775-X	World Almanac Book of World War II, The/Young	$10.95/$14.75 in Canada	
	0-911818-97-9	World Almanac Consumer Information Kit 1986, The	$2.50	
	32187-1	World Almanac Executive Appointment Book 1986, The	$17.95/$24.95 in Canada	
	32628-8	World Almanac Guide to Natural Foods, The/Ross	$8.95/$11.95 in Canada	
	32194-4	World Almanac's Puzzlink™/Considine	$2.95/$3.95 in Canada	
	32626-1	World Almanac's Puzzlink™ 2/Considine	$2.95/$3.95 in Canada	
	31654-X	World Almanac Real Puzzle™ Book, The/Rubin	$2.95/$3.95 in Canada	
	32191-X	World Almanac Real Puzzle™ Book 2, The/Rubin	$2.95/$3.95 in Canada	
	32625-3	World Almanac Real Puzzle™ Book 3, The/Rubin	$2.95/$3.95 in Canada	
		World of Information: see individual titles		

Mail order form to: **World Almanac Publications**
P.O. Box 984
Cincinnati, Ohio 45201

Orders must be prepaid by one of the following methods:
☐ Check or Money Order for _____ attached
☐ Bill my charge card (Add $5.00 processing charge for orders under $20.00)

Order Total_____

Ohio residents add 5.5% sales tax_____

Shipping and Handling:_____
(Add $2.50 for every purchase up to $50.00, and $1.00 for every $10.00 thereafter)

TOTAL PAYMENT_____

Ship to:

Name_____

Street address_____

City/State/Zip Code_____

Special Instructions:_____

_____
Visa Account #   Exp. Date

_____
Master Card Account #   Exp. Date

_____
Interbank #   Exp. Date

_____
Authorized Signature

All orders will be shipped UPS unless otherwise instructed.
We cannot ship C.O.D.